Complete PET

Workbook *with answers*

Peter May and Amanda Thomas

CAMBRIDGE
UNIVERSITY PRESS

CAMBRIDGE
UNIVERSITY PRESS

University Printing House, Cambridge CB2 8BS, United Kingdom

One Liberty Plaza, 20th Floor, New York, NY 10006, USA

477 Williamstown Road, Port Melbourne, VIC 3207, Australia

314–321, 3rd Floor, Plot 3, Splendor Forum, Jasola District Centre, New Delhi – 110025, India

79 Anson Road, #06–04/06, Singapore 079906

Cambridge University Press is part of the University of Cambridge.

It furthers the University's mission by disseminating knowledge in the pursuit of education, learning and research at the highest international levels of excellence.

www.cambridge.org
Information on this title: www.cambridge.org/9780521741408

First published 2010

20 19 18 17 16

Printed in the United Kingdom by Latimer Trend

A catalogue record for this publication is available from the British Library

ISBN 978-0-521-74648-9 Student's Book with CD-ROM
ISBN 978-0-521-74136-1 Student's Book with answers and CD-ROM
ISBN 978-0-521-74139-2 Workbook with Audio CD
ISBN 978-0-521-74140-8 Workbook with answers and Audio CD
ISBN 978-0-521-74137-8 Teacher's Book
ISBN 978-0-521-74138-5 Class Audio CDs (2)
ISBN 978-0-521-74141-5 Student's Book Pack

Contents

Unit 1 Homes and habits

Reading Part 5

Exam advice

The first time you read a Part 5 text, try to guess the missing words – without looking at any of the possible answers A, B, C or D.

Read the text below and choose the correct word for each space.

For each question, mark the correct letter A, B, C or D.

Example:

  0 **A** somebody   **B** everybody   **C** nobody   **D** anybody

Answer: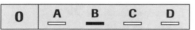

Planning Your Time

Life in the modern world is very busy for almost (0) .... and we all need to plan our time carefully. Possibly the best way to do this is to write a weekly 'to-do' list.

The best time to write your list is (1) .... the weekend. Go somewhere quiet and think about all the things you must do in the (2) .... week. Put them into two groups: first, those you can do any time, such as going to the hairdresser or (3) .... your room. Then think about more (4) .... things, like getting a present for your girlfriend or boyfriend, (5) .... if it's their birthday on Monday!

Decide which things you will do (6) .... which day of the week. Very long lists are not a good idea; it's much better to choose just a (7) .... jobs for Monday and a similar number for the other days of the week.

Early each morning, look at your list. You need to have a plan for the day, (8) .... decide what order you will do everything in. When you finish a job, put a line through it.

You might not complete all your jobs (9) .... day. If it's really impossible to finish doing something, you can add it to your list for the next day, but (10) .... sure you do it first!

1	**A**	in	**B**	by	**C**	for	**D**	at
2	**A**	later	**B**	another	**C**	further	**D**	following
3	**A**	placing	**B**	putting	**C**	tidying	**D**	ordering
4	**A**	urgent	**B**	quick	**C**	sudden	**D**	actual
5	**A**	firstly	**B**	mainly	**C**	generally	**D**	especially
6	**A**	of	**B**	on	**C**	about	**D**	over
7	**A**	few	**B**	couple	**C**	lot	**D**	little
8	**A**	since	**B**	because	**C**	so	**D**	though
9	**A**	some	**B**	every	**C**	both	**D**	any
10	**A**	do	**B**	take	**C**	make	**D**	get

Grammar

Present simple and present continuous

1 ⊙ **Each sentence contains a mistake by a PET candidate. Cross it out and write the correct form.**

1 Hello Stacey, I ~~write~~ to you to say thanks for your letter ....*'m writing*...........

2 That's the best programme on TV and I ~~watching~~ it every night. ....

3 We're going to ~~that~~ cinema because it shows a science-fiction film. ....

4 The weather here is lovely and we stay in a hotel with a big swimming pool. ....

5 In my country people don't ~~wearing~~ clothes like those at weddings. ....

6 I ~~leave~~ this note to let you know which cinema we are going to. ....

7 Every day at school I'm ~~wearing~~ jeans and a black or orange shirt. ....

8 The owners look for someone to work in the shop during the summer. ....

9 He comes from London and is speaking English very well. ....

10 Dear Richard, I send you this email to thank you for your present. ....

2 **Complete the blog with the correct form of the verb in brackets.**

Saturday, January 14   **About me:** Eva, student (Valparaiso, Chile)

Hi, my name is Eva Alonso and I'm 16 years old.

I (1) ....*come*......... (come) from Chile, but I

(2) .... (write) this in Sydney because I

(3) .... (stay) in Australia for the summer.

I (4) .... (live) with a family here, and most

days I (5) .... (go) to a language school for

lessons. The family are very friendly and they always

(6) .... (speak) to me in English, so now

I (7) .... (understand) almost everything.

My pronunciation (8) .... (get) better, too,

but I (9) .... (need) to practise writing

more. I really (10) .... (like) being here and

sometimes I feel that I (11) .... (not want)

to leave, but then I think about my home and my country

and I (12) .... (remember) that it's wonderful

being there, too.

Listening Part 4

Exam advice

Read and listen to the instructions carefully. These often give you useful information such as the topic of the conversation, the names of the speakers, and which of them is female and which male.

Look at the five sentences for this part.
You will hear a conversation between a boy, Leon, and his sister, Zara, about his room.
Decide if each sentence is correct or incorrect.
If it is correct, put a tick (✓) in the box under A for YES. If it is not correct, put a tick (✓) in the box under B for NO.

		A YES	B NO
1	Zara understands why Leon is unhappy with his room.	☐	☐
2	Zara says that his room should be painted white.	☐	☐
3	Zara thinks Leon should get permission before he paints anything.	☐	☐
4	Leon wants to have smaller furniture in the room.	☐	☐
5	Leon and Zara agree that there should be a mirror on the wall.	☐	☐

Writing Part 1

Exam advice

Always check the spelling of each of your completed answers.
If you make a spelling mistake, it will be marked wrong.

Here are some sentences about a new home.
For each question, complete the second sentence so that it means the same as the first.
Use no more than three words.

Example: Our new home is quite near my school.

Our new home is not ......*far from*...... my school.

1 We have a third-floor apartment in a modern building.

Our apartment is ....

the third floor of a modern building.

2 I nearly always walk up the stairs.

I .... ever go up in the lift.

3 There are six rooms in the apartment.

The apartment .... six rooms.

4 There isn't a lot of furniture in my room.

In my room there's only .... furniture.

5 Next weekend we must go shopping!

We must go shopping .... the weekend!

Vocabulary

Complete the puzzle.

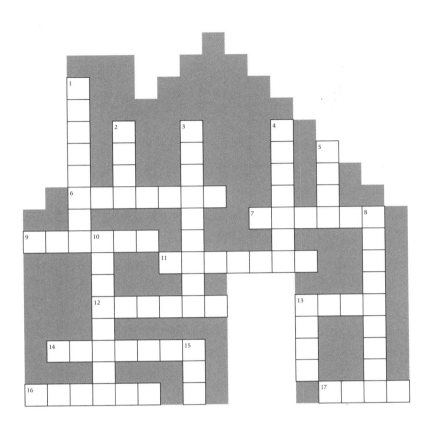

Across

6 I keep my sweaters and socks in a chest of .... in my bedroom.

7 When I'm in bed, I like to have a very soft .... to rest my head on.

9 My parents keep the car in the .... under our block of flats.

11 Our apartment has a .... where you can sit outside and look at the sea.

12 To make meals, I think it's better to use an electric .... rather than a gas one.

13 Before you change a light ...., you should switch off the lamp.

14 I felt hot and I couldn't sleep, so I threw the .... off the bed.

16 When I looked in the ...., I saw that my face was dirty.

17 I put some warm water into the .... and washed the plates and cups.

Down

1 It's a huge house, with a long .... that leads to rooms on the left and right.

2 Three of us sat on the comfortable .... , watching a DVD.

3 Put the food into the .... and it will be cooked in two minutes.

4 I had to sit on a very hard chair for hours, so I put a .... on it.

5 I opened the front door, left my coat in the .... and then went into the living room.

8 I brushed my teeth in the .... next to the bath.

10 My grandfather went to sleep in his .... while he watched TV.

13 Somebody rang the front-door .... and I went to see who was there.

15 I turned off the hot-water .... because the bath was nearly full.

Unit 2 Student days

Listening Part 1

Exam advice
Before you listen, read the questions and look at the pictures. Think about the kind of information you will hear. Then listen, choose the correct picture and put a tick in the box below it.

There are five questions in this part.
For each question there are three pictures and a short recording.
Choose the correct picture and put a tick (✓) in the box below it.

Example: What did the boy use to wear to school?

A ☐   B ☐   C ✓

1 What is included in the cost of the school theatre trip?

A ☐   B ☐   C ☐

2 What time will school finish today?

A ☐   B ☐   C ☐

3 What's the quickest way to get to the boy's school?

A ☐   B ☐   C ☐

4 What must the girl do at 1.30?

A ☐   B ☐   C ☐

5 When will the boy have a maths test?

M	20
T	21
W	22
T	(23)
F	24
S	25
S	26

M	20
T	21
W	22
T	23
F	(24)
S	25
S	26

M	20
T	21
W	22
T	23
F	24
S	(25)
S	26

A ☐   B ☐   C ☐

Reading Part 3

Look at the statements below about two schools.
Read the text to decide if each statement is correct or incorrect.
If it is correct, mark A in the box next to each statement.
If it is not correct, mark B in the box next to each statement.

Exam advice
Read the statements carefully BEFORE you read the text.

A   B

1 Both schools are a short distance from a big city.

2 The City School building was only recently completed.

3 At Heathlands School there are no school fees.

4 Staff and pupils at The City School are happy with the school's facilities.

5 Students at The City School are mainly interested in subjects that will
  help them get a job.

6 At Heathlands School everyone has to study Dance, Drama and Music.

School life: A comparison

Students from two schools, The City School in Nigeria and Heathlands School in the UK, recently took part in a project to compare their education and find out about student life in a very different country. As expected, they found many differences but also a few things that are similar.

The City School is in a district just outside Nigeria's capital, Abuja. The school is surrounded by big trees and grassy fields that the children use to play football on. Heathlands School is in a quiet suburb not far from central Edinburgh, the capital of Scotland.

Most of the 580 students at The City School are taught in pleasant one-storey yellow-brick buildings although some building work still needs to be done. Heathlands School dates from the 1950s but some new facilities have been added recently.

Although The City School receives financial help from the government, students still have to pay school fees. It's hard to find the money sometimes and quite a few parents struggle to keep their children in school. Unlike the Nigerian school, students at Heathlands School only have to buy their uniforms and pay for some extra activities.

Students and teachers at The City School are proud of their library and the science laboratory. They say that there's not a school in the area that can match it. The school concentrates on traditional subjects like Mathematics, Physics and Chemistry because this will make it easier for students to get into a good profession. Practical subjects like Farm Technology are also popular.

Heathlands School recently became a performing arts

college. This means that in addition to subjects like English and Mathematics, the school also offers lessons in Dance, Drama and Music as options for all students. There is a new dance studio which can also be used as a theatre.

Students in both schools found the project very interesting and hope to do further joint projects in the future.

Vocabulary

Complete the sentences with the correct form of the verbs in the box. You need to use some words more than once.

take	make	spend	miss	lose
learn	study	fail	have	

1   I .... my Maths exam, so I'll have to .... it again next term.

2   I'm not sure what I want to .... at university but I don't have to .... a decision about it yet.

3   This morning I was late, so I .... my History class. I had to .... all my break time copying my friend's notes.

4   I .... a lot of fun on the Drama course last summer. I .... so many friends.

5   Tonight I need to .... for the test. If I don't answer every question, I will .... marks.

6   Every week our English teacher gives us a list of words to .... She says if we .... ten minutes doing this every day, we'll remember them more easily.

7   I don't .... much money on books as I can .... them out of the school library.

8   If you .... the school bus, it will .... you a long time to walk.

9   Yesterday I .... my school bag. I've looked everywhere but I can't find it.

10 My mum .... a good suggestion yesterday. She thinks I should earn some money by teaching English to young children.

Grammar

Past simple, Past continuous, *used to*

❶ Choose the correct form of the verb.

1   When I was younger I *used to go / was going* to school by bus.

2   I *wasn't / didn't* allowed to watch TV while I *used to do / was doing* my homework.

3   When you *were phoning / phoned* me yesterday I *used to walk / was walking* home from my friend's house.

4   Last Friday while I *studied / was studying*, the baby next door *cried / was crying*. It was very noisy so I had to go to the library in town.

5   I *was meeting / met* my best friend while I *used to wait / was waiting* for the bus.

6   I *didn't finish / wasn't finishing* my homework because I *didn't listen / wasn't listening* when my teacher explained what we had to do.

7   I *wasn't liking / didn't use to like* Maths but now I think it's really interesting.

8   When we *played / were playing* our hockey match I *was falling over / fell over* three times.

❷ Complete the questions with one word and match them to the answers.

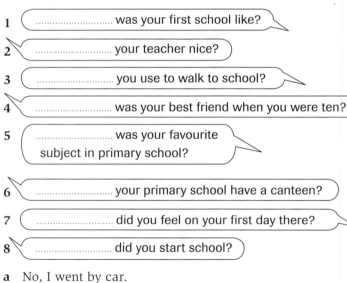

1   .... was your first school like?

2   .... your teacher nice?

3   .... you use to walk to school?

4   .... was your best friend when you were ten?

5   .... was your favourite subject in primary school?

6   .... your primary school have a canteen?

7   .... did you feel on your first day there?

8   .... did you start school?

a   No, I went by car.

b   Her name was Mary.

c   She was very strict.

d   I was very nervous.

e   When I was four years old.

f   I liked PE/sports best.

g   It was quite small but it had a big playground.

h   No, we had to eat in the school hall.

Writing Part 2

❶ Read this exam task.

An English friend of yours called Sam is ill and couldn't play in a school basketball match yesterday, which your team lost.

Write an email to Sam. In your email you should

- apologise for not phoning him after the match
- explain why you think your team lost
- offer to visit him soon.

Write **35–45 words**.

Exam advice

Remember you can only write 35–45 words. Do not include unnecessary information.

❷ Look at the content points carefully. Tick the pieces of information that you could include in the email.

a a reason why you didn't phone after the match ☐

b a question about Sam's health ☐

c where the basketball match was ☐

d what the score was ☐

e a description of the other team ☐

f who you sat next to at the match ☐

g a description of how your team played ☐

h a suggestion about when you can go to his house ☐

i an invitation to your house ☐

j a message for Sam from some of your friends ☐

❸ Look at this student's answer. Is all the information included for each content point? Is there any unnecessary information?

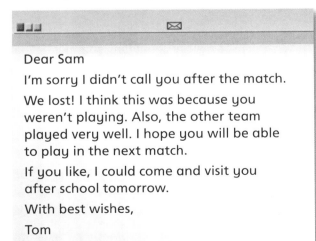

Dear Sam

I'm sorry I didn't call you after the match.

We lost! I think this was because you weren't playing. Also, the other team played very well. I hope you will be able to play in the next match.

If you like, I could come and visit you after school tomorrow.

With best wishes,

Tom

❹ Now use the following checklist to find any other problems with the email.

Writing Part 2 Checklist

Is the email the right length? ☐

Is the email addressed to the right person? ☐

Is any of the language too formal or informal? ☐

Are there appropriate phrases for explaining, inviting, suggesting, etc? ☐

Are the right tenses used? ☐

Are there any spelling errors? ☐

❺ Make any changes you think are necessary to the message.

❻ Yesterday you arranged to go shopping with an English friend called Anna but you had a problem and couldn't go.

Write an email to Anna. In your email you should

- apologise and explain what happened
- ask about Anna's shopping trip
- suggest something else to do together.

Write **35–45 words**.

Unit 3 Fun time

End of the summer holidays?

In many countries, schools have long summer holidays, with shorter holidays in between. However, a new report suggests reducing the length of school holidays to stop children forgetting what they have learnt during the long summer break. Instead of three school terms, it says, there should be five eight-week terms. There would be just four weeks off in the summer, with a two-week break between the other terms. The annual amount of holiday time would remain the same.

Sonia Montero has two children at primary school and works full time. She supports the idea. 'The kids,' she says, 'have much longer holidays than me and I can't afford to take several weeks off work, so I need someone to take care of them. But nobody wants the work in the summer months – they all have holidays of their own.'

Not surprisingly, some young people disagree. Student Jason Panos, 15, says: 'It's a stupid idea. I really can't imagine staying at school in the summer – I'd hate it. It's totally unfair, too. The people who suggest this had long school holidays when they were young, but now they want to stop us enjoying the summer. They only need to look at places like Spain and America, where they have much longer holidays than here. The kids there don't forget everything they've learnt in a couple of months, do they?'

Nadia Salib, 14, agrees. 'Sure,' she says, 'the first week at school after the summer is never easy, but you soon get back into it. The real problem round here is that kids get bored after so many weeks out of school, and then some of them start causing trouble. But the answer is to give them something to do in their free time, not make everyone stay in school longer. We'd all hate that.'

Reading Part 4

Exam advice
Before you make your final choice of answer, find reasons in the text *why* the other three options are wrong.

Read the text and the questions below. For each question, mark the correct letter A, B, C or D.

1 Why is Sonia in favour of shorter school holidays?
   A She can't get anyone to mind her children in summer.
   B She thinks that secondary school holidays are too long.
   C She can't afford to pay someone to look after her children.
   D She doesn't get any summer holidays in her present job.

2 What does Jason say about long summer holidays?
   A They can help children forget about school.
   B They have no effect on children's education.
   C These days many older people have them too.
   D Schools in other countries don't have them.

3 What does Nadia say about young people in summer?
   A They behave badly when they go back to school.
   B Long holidays are very bad for their education.
   C They would like to spend more time at school.
   D Where she lives there is nothing for them to do.

4 Which of the following emails best explains the article?

A
They've changed all the school terms and some students are getting very angry about it.

B
Some people want to change the school year but not everyone thinks it's a good idea.

C
Everyone's against the idea of shortening the summer holidays so they've decided to forget the idea.

D
Teenagers are very worried because there are going to be fewer school holidays in the year.

Grammar

verbs + *-ing*/infinitive

❶ (•) Each sentence contains a mistake by a PET candidate. Cross it out and write the correct *–ing* or infinitive form of the verb.

1 I hope hearing from you soon. ....*to hear*............

2 Would you mind to lend me your bicycle?

....

3 In the afternoon, if it's possible, I want play beach volleyball. ....

4 I love Florence, so I suggest to spend much more time there. ....

5 It's my favourite movie, but I couldn't afford buying the DVD before. ....

6 Our new teacher seems be very good.

....

7 I apologise because I couldn't avoid to miss the class. ....

8 I feel like stay at home today. ....

9 I just need your tent for two days' camping and I promise taking care of it. ....

10 The beach is next to the hotel and there are courses to learn doing water sports.

....

❷ Tick the correct sentences. Correct the sentences which are wrong.

1 **a** The small boat began to go faster and faster as we approached the waterfall. ☐

   b Next month I want to begin doing dancing lessons. ☐

2 **a** Please remember bringing some money tomorrow. ☐

   b I'll remember to send you a text message when I arrive. ☐

3 **a** My brother often forgets turning off the lights when he goes out. ☐

   b I'm sorry but I completely forgot buying bread at the shops. ☐

4 **a** I really like spending time sightseeing in different countries. ☐

   b Alfie doesn't like to go camping in the winter. ☐

5 **a** I remember to go to Disneyland when I was a child. ☐

   b Do you remember to watch that great film last month? ☐

6 **a** Jessica says she forgets going into that shop, but I saw her there. ☐

   b I'll never forget to see my team win last year's Cup Final. ☐

Listening Part 2

You will hear an interview with Ben Lacey, who collects postcards.
For each question, put a tick (✓) in the correct box.

1   Ben first became interested in postcards when

    A   he found a collection at home. ☐

    B   he was on a family holiday. ☐

    C   he began travelling on his own. ☐

2   Who else in the family collected postcards?

    A   Ben's grandfather ☐

    B   Ben's uncle ☐

    C   Ben's mother ☐

3   Ben's favourite postcards have pictures of

    A   ways people used to travel. ☐

    B   very well-known ports. ☐

    C   lovely religious buildings. ☐

4   He says that some old postcards are amusing because

    A   the jokes on them are very funny. ☐

    B   they show old-fashioned attitudes. ☐

    C   they are extremely badly drawn. ☐

5   The postcards that are worth most

    A   are over 100 years old. ☐

    B   have never been used. ☐

    C   show particular scenes. ☐

6   Ben suggests new collectors should get

    A   many different kinds of cards. ☐

    B   cards showing their own town. ☐

    C   cards that have sports pictures. ☐

Writing Part 1

Exam advice
Sometimes more than one answer in this part is possible but you should only write one answer for each question.

**Here are some sentences about camping.
For each question, complete the second sentence
so that it means the same as the first.
Use no more than three words.**

Example:

Last year I started to go camping with my friends.

I took ....*up*........ camping with my friends last year.

1   It's really wonderful to breathe fresh air in the countryside.

    I really enjoy .... fresh air in the countryside.

2   Thinking about my next camping trip is always exciting.

    I always look .... my next camping trip.

3   We don't usually go camping when it's very cold.

    When it's very cold, we usually avoid .... camping.

4   Some campsites are too expensive for us.

    We can't .... stay in some campsites.

5   I like camping much more than staying in hotels.

    I much .... to staying in hotels.

Vocabulary

Read the clues and complete the crossword.

Across

2   person who rides a bicycle
4   hard hat to protect the head
6   amount of money you pay
7   move around the Internet
10 reserve tickets, holidays, etc.
11 person who makes a meal
12 swim under the water
13 physically strong and well

Down

1   what something is worth
2   board game played on squares
3   where campers sleep
5   have enough money for
6   want to have or do something
8   short name for 'bicycle'
9   object used for taking photos
10 object used for painting

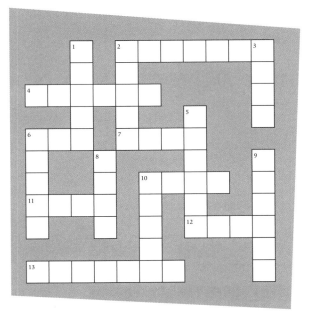

Unit 4　Our world

Reading Part 3

Exam advice

Make sure you underline the parts of the text which give you the answers.

Look at the statements below about a tour in Norway.
Read the text below to decide if each statement is correct or incorrect.
If it is correct, mark A in the box. If it is not correct, mark B in the box.

		A	B
1	The majority of Sami people live in Norway.	☐	☐
2	A bus takes you all the way from Tromsø to Karasjok.	☐	☐
3	You will learn to sing special songs called *Joik*.	☐	☐
4	You are likely to see the Northern Lights if the weather conditions are good.	☐	☐
5	You have to pay extra to do the optional activities.	☐	☐
6	The special swimming suit allows you to swim under the ice in the Barents Sea.	☐	☐
7	On the Reindeer Sled Ride, a guide will drive the reindeer.	☐	☐
8	People of all ages can do the optional activities.	☐	☐

Winter Adventure in Norway

This new tour takes you up to the far north of Norway, deep inside the Arctic Circle, to meet the Sami people and find out about their way of life. The Sami people live in four countries: Norway, Sweden, Finland and Russia. There are about 70,000 Sami in total with around 40,000 in Norway, 20,000 in Sweden, 6,000 in Finland and 2,000 in Russia.

The voyage begins in the port of Tromsø, in Norway. You travel from here to Karasjok in the heart of Norwegian Lapland, or Sapmi, as the Sami call it. The journey starts on board *The North Cape*, cruising along the wild and unspoilt coast to Kirknes, which is located just 10km from the Russian border, and continues by bus inland to Karasjok.

During our two-night stay in Karasjok you will visit the Sami Cultural Park to learn about the history and the future of the Sami and enjoy the rare opportunity to listen to the Sami traditional singing, known as *Joik*. Also included is an evening walk wearing snow shoes in search of the Northern Lights. If the skies are clear there is a good chance you will be rewarded with a spectacular display as waves of colour fill the night sky.

Reindeer Sled Ride

There will also be the chance to do some optional half-day trips (additional prices available on request):

- **Bathing in the Barents Sea**
  Snowmobiles transport you to the Barents Sea, and with special survival suits to keep you warm, you can enjoy the unique experience of floating in the icy waters. Hot tea and a sauna are available after your swim.

- **Reindeer Sled Ride**
  This magical experience is one you will never forget. The reindeer sled ride will take you along old Sami paths where you can enjoy the peace and silence of the ancient forest. Each sled takes two people and you can take it in turns to guide the reindeer.

- **Cross-country skiing**
  This is the national sport of Norway and a wonderful way to experience the beauty of the landscape and get some exercise at the same time.

Please note – these optional trips are only suitable for children of 12 years and over.

On the final day you will travel by bus to Lakely airport for your return flight home.

Listening Part 3

Exam advice

Before you listen, look at the notes about the sightseeing tour. What type of information is missing? Try to think of some possible answers for each gap.

You will hear a tour guide giving some information to a group of students.

For each question, fill in the missing information in the numbered space.

San Francisco Sightseeing Tour

Leave hotel at **(1)** .... - ferry leaves at 10am.

May need a **(2)** ....

Sausalito:

An opportunity to go **(3)** ....

Golden Gate Park

De Young Museum:

Must see the collection of **(4)** .... from USA.

OR

Japanese Tea Garden:

dates from **(5)** ....

Lunch

See famous **(6)** .... in Alamo Square. Walk around Chinatown.

Grammar

Comparative and superlative adjectives

❶ Does the second sentence have the same meaning as the first sentence? Tick the correct box. Rewrite any second sentences which have a different meaning, so that they mean the same as the first sentence.

1 There is no other city in Europe as big as Moscow.

   Moscow isn't the biggest city in Europe.

   ☐ Same   ☐ Different

2 Rome isn't quite as cold as Paris.

   Paris is a little colder than Rome.

   ☐ Same   ☐ Different

3 Shanghai is one of the world's busiest ports.

   There are many ports in the world that are as busy as Shanghai.

   ☐ Same   ☐ Different

4 The CN tower in Toronto is much smaller than the Burj Dubai.

   The Burj Dubai is as tall as the CN tower.

   ☐ Same   ☐ Different

5 It's more expensive to live on Avenue Princess Grace in Monaco than on Fifth Avenue in New York.

   You need to pay as much to live on Avenue Princess Grace as on Fifth Avenue.

   ☐ Same   ☐ Different

6 Up to 9.5 million tourists visit Singapore every year.

   As many as 9.5 million tourists visit Singapore every year.

   ☐ Same   ☐ Different

❷ **Complete the sentences with the correct form of the adjective in brackets.**

1 Flying is still the .... (safe) way to travel.

2 Howler monkeys are much .... (noisy) than elephants.

3 San Francisco is one of the .... (hilly) cities in the world.

4 October is the .... (good) time to see whales in Argentina.

5 A hippopotamus is .... (heavy) than a rhinoceros.

6 Istanbul is as .... (big) as London.

7 Travelling by train is much .... (good) for the environment.

8 Vancouver is .... (far) from São Paolo than Paris.

9 The city of Cherrapunji in India is the .... (wet) in the world.

10 Bears are as .... (dangerous) as lions.

Vocabulary

❶ **Complete the sentences with an adjective from the box. You do not need to use all the adjectives.**

| warm | filthy | fantastic | terrible | boring | crowded |
| noisy | expensive | freezing | fascinating | cheap | |

Katie: What did you think of the hotel? I thought it was quite nice.

Hannah: Really? I thought the food was absolutely (1) .... !

Katie: I enjoyed going to the museum. I found it really (2) ....

Hannah: Oh no! I thought it was extremely (3) ....

Katie: I got some quite (4) .... things in the market.

Hannah: I didn't buy anything. It was much too (5) ....

Katie: Did you go swimming in the sea? The water was really (6) ....

Hannah: When I went it was absolutely (7) .... !

Katie: There weren't too many people at the beach though, were there?

Hannah: Actually, it seemed quite (8) .... to me.

Katie: I really liked walking in the streets in the evening. Everywhere was so clean and modern.

Hannah: What do you mean? The streets were absolutely (9) .... !

Katie: Well, I'm sorry you didn't enjoy it. I had a (10) .... holiday!

❷ **Put the adjectives from Exercise 1 into the table below. You need to use each adjective at least twice.**

very	really	absolutely	extremely

❸ **Complete the sentences so they are true for you.**

1 .... is an extremely boring place.

2 The most expensive thing I've ever bought was ....

3 I'd recommend .... for an absolutely fantastic holiday.

4 .... is a really fascinating place to visit.

5 The weather in .... is absolutely terrible.

6 .... is an extremely expensive shop.

4 **Put the letters in the correct order and match the places to the definitions.**

1 lipoec taoinst

....

2 thyou bluc

....

3 msutdia

....

4 yroctfa

....

5 rtisout cefifo

....

6 tra yllager

....

a This is where visitors to a town can get maps and information.

b This is where you can see paintings and sculptures.

c This is where you go to watch football matches and other sporting events.

d This a place where teenagers can go to make new friends.

e This is where you go if someone steals something from you.

f This is where products are made, like cars for example.

Writing Part 3

1 **This is part of a letter you receive from an English penfriend.**

> Tell me about your favourite kind of holiday. What do you do every day? Why do you like it?

Look at this student's answer, read the questions below and tick YES or NO.

Dear Harry

My favourite kind of holiday is skiing.
I like going to the mountains in Austria.
I go there every year with my family.
We stay in an apartment near the ski lift.
Every day I go snowboarding with my dad and my brother. We have races and I usually win. My dad is always the slowest. My mum skis with my little sister. Snowboarding is fun. I like the views from the top of the mountains. The mountain air is good. I like it better than a holiday at the beach.
What about you?

From Stephan

Does Stephan ...	Yes	No
a give all the necessary information?	☐	☐
b start and end the letter in a suitable way?	☐	☐
c use enough long sentences with connecting words (e.g. *like, which, because*)?	☐	☐
d use a variety of different structures?	☐	☐
e use some interesting vocabulary?	☐	☐

(•) **Stephan says: 'My favourite kind of holiday is skiing.' Another way to say this is: 'The kind of holiday I enjoy the most is skiing.' Sometimes PET candidates write 'My preferite holiday' or 'My best holiday', which are wrong.**

2 **Now you write a letter to your penfriend about your favourite kind of holiday. Write about 100 words.**

Make sure you don't make the same mistakes as Stephan.

Unit 5 Feelings

Reading Part 5

Exam advice

Never leave an answer in Part 5 – or any other part of Reading – blank. If you really don't know which letter to choose, guess. You don't lose marks for a wrong answer, but you can't get a mark if you don't put anything.

Read the text below and choose the correct word for each space. For each question, mark the correct letter A, B, C or D.

Example:

0 A anybody   **B** somebody   **C** everybody   **D** nobody

Answer:

0	A	B	C	D

Making Friends

You may think that (0) .... knows how to make friends, but for some people it isn't so easy. (1) .... they want to be friends with others, they always seem to be alone. Sadly, some of them get depressed (2) .... this.

We wanted to find out how these people can make friends, (3) .... we asked a group of 14-year-olds what sort of people they prefer. The most important thing, they said, is that they can get (4) .... with them. They like to be friends with kind and generous people, who rarely get angry (5) .... others. They also like people who laugh at their jokes, and can tell (6) .... stories, too. They (7) .... be interested in what the group does, and perhaps even think of (8) .... new things to do.

We also asked the group how not to make friends with them. Here are some of the things they mention: always telling others what they (9) .... to do, telling lies about people, and talking about themselves (10) .... the time!

1	**A**	Although	**B**	Even	**C**	Despite	**D**	However
2	**A**	for	**B**	about	**C**	of	**D**	under
3	**A**	since	**B**	because	**C**	so	**D**	as
4	**A**	on	**B**	down	**C**	back	**D**	in
5	**A**	to	**B**	against	**C**	with	**D**	by
6	**A**	amused	**B**	cheerful	**C**	smiling	**D**	funny
7	**A**	can	**B**	ought	**C**	need	**D**	should
8	**A**	annoying	**B**	exciting	**C**	embarrassing	**D**	disappointing
9	**A**	have	**B**	could	**C**	may	**D**	must
10	**A**	most	**B**	all	**C**	every	**D**	only

Vocabulary
adjectives ending in -ed/-ing

① (•) **Some of these sentences written by PET candidates have mistakes. Correct the errors.**

1 My best friend sent me an email with an ~~interested~~ story. ......*interesting*......

2 My room is very big and there is a TV, so I won't feel boring at night. ....

3 He was so tired he fell asleep as soon as he arrived home. ....

4 It's an amazing story and in my opinion, it is a great book. ....

5 The film is extremely excited. ....

6 I was really surprised when I read the email.
....

7 The music is so nice and it makes you feel relaxing. ....

8 I would like to see that thriller because I like frightened films. ....

9 I was very unhappy and embarrassed at that moment. ....

10 The airline lost my suitcase, so I felt very annoying. ....

Adjectives describing how people feel

② **ⓐ** **Complete the puzzle with adjectives. The letters down form another word.**

1 happy, and showing it
2 worried about, or afraid of, something
3 very unhappy, often for a long time
4 happy because nothing is worrying you
5 feeling happy about your life and future
6 feeling unhappy about your life and future
7 very pleased about something that has happened
8 unhappy because something wasn't as good as you hoped

1 C H E E R F U L
2 _ _ _ _ _ _
3 _ _ _ _ _ _ _
4 _ _ _ _ _
5 _ _ _ _ _ _
6 _ _ _ _ _ _ _
7 _ _ _ _ _ _ _
8 _ _ _ _ _ _ _ _ _

ⓑ **Put the words into four pairs of opposite meanings.**

Listening Part 4

Look at the six sentences for this part.
You will hear a conversation between a girl, Holly, and a boy, Max, about having a party.
Decide if each sentence is correct or incorrect.
If it is correct, put a tick in the box under A for YES. If it is not correct, put a tick in the box under B for NO.

	A YES	B NO
1 Holly thinks Max should invite people this week.	☐	☐
2 Max wants to invite more than twenty people.	☐	☐
3 Max says all his friends have a lot in common.	☐	☐
4 Holly says Max should buy some new CDs for the party.	☐	☐
5 Holly and Max share the same opinion about playing a DVD.	☐	☐
6 In the end, Holly persuades Max to have the party on a Friday.	☐	☐

Grammar
modals

1 Make this dialogue sound more natural by replacing expressions 1–10 with forms of *should, must, have to, can* and *might*. Add pronouns like *we* where necessary. In one case two answers are possible.

Example:
I don't think <u>it's possible for us to</u> get tickets.
we can

Sam: If (1) <u>it's impossible for us to</u> go out tonight, let's go somewhere tomorrow.

Alex: Yes, I think (2) <u>it would be a good idea for us to</u> have an evening in the town centre.

Sam: OK, but only for a few hours. (3) <u>I'm not allowed to</u> stay out very late.

Alex: Well, (4) <u>it's possible we won't</u> be back until half past ten.

Sam: That's all right. (5) <u>It isn't necessary for me to</u> be back before eleven.

Alex: So where do you think (6) <u>it would be best to</u> go?

Sam: How about that new nightclub? (7) <u>It's possible it's</u> open tomorrow.

Alex: It's very expensive. Let's go somewhere (8) <u>it's unnecessary to</u> pay.

Sam: No, thanks.

Alex: Perhaps (9) <u>it would be a mistake for us to</u> go out tomorrow, after all.

Sam: Maybe (10) <u>it would be a good idea for me to</u> go out with someone else!

2 Circle the correct modal in each sentence.

1 Hannah *may* / *can* / *might* ski really well and she often wins competitions.

2 I *might* / *can* / *couldn't* go to the party but I'm still not sure.

3 This is our secret, so you *mightn't* / *mustn't* / *don't have to* tell anyone else.

4 It's dangerous to go into deep water if you *mightn't* / *can't* / *may not* swim.

5 I think you *must* / *should* / *have to* go out more and meet new people.

6 I don't feel very well so I *may* / *can* / *have to* stay in tonight.

7 You *don't have to* / *mustn't* / *mightn't* come with us if you don't want to.

8 Passengers *ought to* / *must* / *should* remain in their seats while the plane is landing.

9 *May* / *Must* / *Could* you please phone me in the evening?

10 To get a driving licence, you *may* / *should* / *have to* be 18 or over.

3 Tick the sentences that are correct. Rewrite the incorrect sentences. In some cases more than one modal is possible. Three sentences are correct.

1 I may go out later with my friends, but I'm not sure.

2 There's a lot of traffic today so the bus has to arrive late.

3 Students might not talk during the written exam.

4 Paula plays the piano and she can sing quite well, too.

5 You ought to wear a uniform when you're in the army.

6 Children don't have to eat too much ice cream.

7 There may not be time to go to the shops because they close soon.

8 Yes, you can go out tonight but you might be home no later than 11pm.

9 I'm on holiday now so I mustn't get up early. It's great!

10 I haven't got my watch on, but I think it can be about 6.30 now.

Writing Part 3 (letter)

❶ Quickly read the question and the student's answer in Exercise 2 below. Has she answered all parts of the question? What do you notice about the style of the letter?

This is part of a letter you receive from an English penfriend.

> Last Saturday I had a party for all my friends. We had a fantastic time! Tell me about parties in your country. What are they like? What do people do?

Now write a letter answering your penfriend's questions. Write your **letter** in about 100 words.

❷ Now read the letter more carefully. Replace the unsuitable expressions with more informal words, as in the example. Choose from this list:

Well, that's all for now	Best wishes	Sorry
Please write soon	Thanks for	great!

~~Dear Sir~~, Hi Freddie

I have received your letter. I apologise to you for not writing sooner, but I've been really busy lately.

Your party sounds extremely enjoyable. Here, parties are normally for family and friends. The men usually wear their best suits and the women have long dresses on, though nowadays many young people just wear what they like.

There's always plenty of nice food, including a delicious cake. Everyone has lots of fun together, chatting, laughing and – later on – dancing. Sometimes, especially in summer, the party goes on most of the night!

I have no further information to add at the present time. I look forward to hearing from you.

Yours sincerely,
Ruby

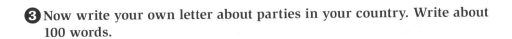

❸ Now write your own letter about parties in your country. Write about 100 words.

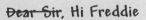

Unit 6 Leisure and fashion

Reading Part 2

Exam advice

It's a good idea to <u>underline</u> where you find your answer in the DVD Guide to make sure you have found the most important points.

The people below all want to rent a DVD to watch.
On the opposite page there are reviews of eight films.
Decide which film would be most suitable for each person.

1  Luke plays the guitar really well and wants to be a musician. His parents have recommended this film because it's by a very good director and it also shows what the music business is like.

2  Daniel's interests are history and travel. He likes films with an exciting story and plenty of action. Tonight he wants to watch a movie with his girlfriend, who is studying Old English literature.

3  Alicia wants to rent a DVD to watch with her family. The children enjoy stories about animals that have a happy ending. Alicia's husband is interested in films that are about things that really happen.

4  Eric wants to watch a DVD with his 14 year-old grandson who loves sport and music. Eric likes films which have a positive message and which make you feel better.

5  Sophie and her friends are doing a film-studies project on films for teenagers. They are interested in romantic comedies about relationships between people of their own age.

DVD guide: REVIEWS

A The Commitments

Based on Roddy Doyle's novel, *The Commitments* is a hugely stylish movie, expertly directed by the great Alan Parker. What makes it special is that Parker chose unknown teenagers to play the main characters. The story begins when Jimmy Rabitte decides to bring the sound of the great 1960's soul singers to Dublin by creating a band.

B Cinema Paradiso

This tells the story of Salvatore, a successful movie director, who returns to the Sicilian village where he grew up. Salvatore remembers his childhood and how he developed his love for the cinema at the local cinema, Cinema Paradiso. The film illustrates the importance of the cinema for the local community; how it helped them escape from all the problems of daily life in post-war Italy.

C Beowulf and Grendel

Danish hero, Beowulf, comes to help King Hrothgar fight the monster Grendel. Based on the 8th century poem, the film has a great atmosphere, excellent costumes and sets, and some good performances, which together bring this well-known legend to life.

D Belleville Rendez-vous

Champion, a boy who loves cycling and hopes to win the Tour de France, is taken prisoner by a gang of criminals. His grandmother and her dog, Bruno, set out on a dangerous adventure to rescue the boy. This beautifully filmed cartoon gives a touching and believable account of what a dog's life is like.

E The Adventures of Greyfriar's Bobby

The Adventures of Greyfriar's Bobby is a wonderful story about friendship between animals and people. Based on a true story in which a young boy called Ewan tries to look after Bobby, who doesn't understand when his owner dies. Ewan wins the trust of Bobby and finds a new best friend.

F Gregory's Girl

Tall, lacking in confidence and unsure of his feelings, Gregory sets out to win the heart of Dorothy. Dorothy is in the same class at school and unfortunately is much better at football than Gregory. Set in Scotland in the late 1970s, this sweet, funny, warm film shows exactly what it's like to be in love for the first time. This is first class and superbly directed.

G Iqbal

Iqbal is about having the courage to follow your dreams. It follows the story of an 18-year-old deaf boy from a poor family living in India, who is determined to play for the Indian national cricket team. This is heart-warming entertainment at its best, even if it's a bit unrealistic.

H The City of Lost Children

This is set in a fantasy world where a mad scientist tries to steal the dreams of children. French directors Marc Caro and Jean-Pierre Jeunet succeed in creating a frightening magical world with unforgettable characters and scenery. The weird circus music also adds to the strange atmosphere. There are some excellent performances from the young actors.

Vocabulary

1 Put the letters in the correct order. The first letter of each word is given.

1 I decided not to go and see the film because I read a bad (V E R I W E) r _ _ _ _ _ of it.

2 I don't enjoy watching films with (T I L U S T E S B) s _ _ _ _ _ _ _ _ . I can't read them fast enough!

3 The play was really boring and some people didn't stay to see the end. They left during the (N T R E L V A I) i _ _ _ _ _ _ _ _

4 The band gave a great (N E C E A F P R M O R) p _ _ _ _ _ _ _ _ _ _ last night.

5 The sports stadium is a good (E X N E U) v _ _ _ _ _ for a big concert because it has thousands of seats.

6 Sometimes seeing your favourite band (V L E I) l _ _ _ is disappointing because the sound isn't very good.

7 There's a music festival on this weekend and (M D A S I S I N O) a _ _ _ _ _ _ _ _ is free!

8 The play was very sad. A lot of the people in the (D E I N U A C E) a _ _ _ _ _ _ _ were crying.

② Write the missing vowels for the
names of the TV programmes.

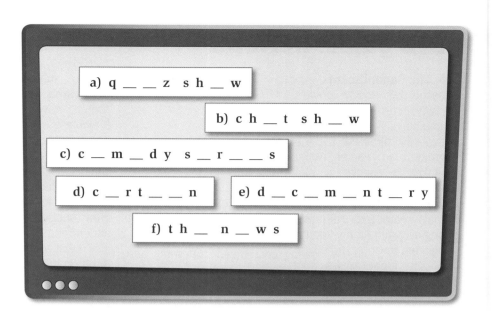

a) q _ _ z s h _ w

b) c h _ t s h _ w

c) c _ m _ d y s _ r _ _ s

d) c _ r t _ _ n

e) d _ c _ m _ n t _ r y

f) t h _ n _ w s

Listening Part 1

Exam advice
Think of the words to describe each picture before you listen.

There are five questions. For each question there are
three pictures and a short recording.
Choose the correct picture and put a tick (✓) below it.

Example:
What did the boy use to wear to school?

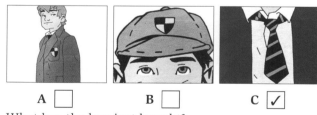

A ☐   B ☐   C ✓

1   What has the boy just bought?

A ☐   B ☐   C ☐

2   What does Rachel need to get for the party?

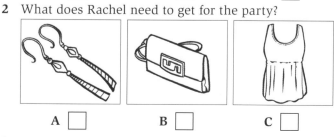

A ☐   B ☐   C ☐

3   What is Kerry wearing?

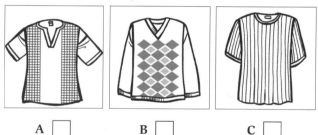

A ☐   B ☐   C ☐

4   What does the reviewer recommend on TV this evening?

A ☐   B ☐   C ☐

5   What time does the film start?

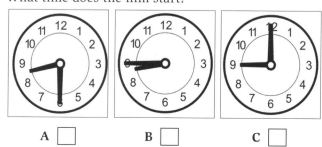

A ☐   B ☐   C ☐

Grammar

Present perfect and past simple

❶ Choose the correct word to fill each space.

| since | for | already | yet | just |

1 I've played the piano .... two years.

2 Emma doesn't want to watch that film because she's .... seen it. She saw it in the cinema when it first came out.

3 It's difficult to get tickets for the play at The King's Theatre because it's only .... opened.

4 I haven't been to the circus .... I was six years old.

5 They haven't finished making the new *Spider's* album ....

6 You don't need to book the cinema tickets. I've .... done it. I got them last night.

7 I've .... started a dance course. I've only had one lesson so far but I really enjoyed it.

8 Have you seen the news .... ?

9 The band haven't played together .... a long time, so they're feeling very nervous.

10 That show has been on TV .... 1978!

❷ Complete the sentences with the correct tense of the verb in brackets, using the past simple or present perfect.

1 I .... (stay) up all night to finish the exciting book I was reading.

2 Mark .... (not decide) if he's going to the party on Saturday yet.

3 Annie .... (read) that book when she was ten.

4 Sam and Jake .... (visit) New York twice.

5 Last night I .... (watch) a really interesting documentary on TV.

6 My mum and dad .... (know) each other for twenty years.

7 I .... (not wear) that dress since last summer. Now it's too short.

8 Sophie was a journalist before she .... (become) a teacher.

Writing Part 2

❶ (•) In Writing Part 2 you often have to make suggestions and offers. Look at these examples of students' writing.

a I suggest us to see *Twilight*.

b I suggest seeing *Twilight*.

c I suggest you this film because it's interesting.

d What about seeing *Twilight*?

e Let's see *Twilight*?

f I offer you to book the tickets.

g Shall I book the tickets?

h I can get the tickets if you want.

Which sentence(s)

- are grammatically incorrect? ....

- has a punctuation mistake? ....

- are OK? ....

Can you think of any other phrases for making suggestions and offers?

❷ Look at this exam task.

An English friend of yours called Isabel wants to go to the cinema with you this weekend.

Write an email to Isabel. In your email you should:

- suggest which film to see
- explain why you want to see it
- offer to book the tickets.

Write **35–45 words.**

Now you write the email to Isabel.

❸ Check your work using the checklist.

Is your email the right length? ☐

Is your email addressed to the right person? ☐

Are there appropriate phrases for

suggesting? .... ☐

explaining? .... ☐

offering? .... ☐

Are there any spelling or punctuation errors? ☐

Unit 7 Out and about

Reading Part 1

Look at the text in each question.
What does it say?
Mark the correct letter A, B or C.

Example:

> ## DVD suitable only for persons of 15 years and over.

A You shouldn't watch this if you're 14.

B You have to be 16 to watch this.

C You won't enjoy watching this if you're 18.

Example answer: A

1

> **Free** travel on buses and trams for young people in full-time education.

A There is no charge for students on public transport.

B No young people have to pay on public transport.

C Students can travel free only to and from school.

2

> Tickets **must** be bought before boarding trains. **All** platforms have ticket machines.

A You can get a ticket on the train.

B You have to get a ticket in the station.

C You must get a ticket before you go to the station.

3

> **To:** Liam
>
> **From:** Nicole
>
> Plane delayed by fog. Unless the flight is cancelled, we'll take the train after we land there.

Nicole tells Liam that they will

A definitely go by plane and then train.

B go by train instead of taking the plane.

C take the train if they arrive by plane.

4

> **For the safety of children, bikes are *not* allowed in this area.**

A Cyclists should ride carefully here.

B You must not ride bicycles here.

C Only adults may ride bicycles here.

5

> **MESSAGE**
>
> Jake – Louis phoned. He wonders if you can call in on your way home and help him with his homework.
> Tilly

What does Louis want Jake to do?

A phone him about his homework

B do his homework with him

C do all his homework for him

Grammar

The future: *will, going to*, present continuous, present simple

❶ (•) Some of these sentences written by PET candidates have mistakes. Correct the errors.

1 I need to go now, because my lesson starts in ten minutes.
2 I go to buy a bigger wardrobe tomorrow.
3 I'm sorry, but I don't will be in the English class tomorrow.
4 What I'm going to do during these holidays?
5 I think I'll take part in the dancing competition but I'm not sure.
6 You didn't going to believe this, but I didn't have any problems.
7 I hope that the weather shall be better at the end of the week.
8 I'm not going to be able to come tomorrow because I have a doctor's appointment.
9 There's a movie on tonight, so we'll meet everyone at Carla's house at 7 pm.
10 I think I'm going to buy some flowers to make my room more beautiful.

❷ Read Jessica's letter and choose the correct form of the verbs in bold.

Hi Amelia,

Well, here we are in Athens, in sunny Greece! The TV weather forecast says it (1) **is reaching / is going to reach** 40°C later today, so we'd better go out soon to look round the city before it (2) **gets / will get** too hot!

We spoke to some friends last night and we (3) **'ll meet / 're meeting** them at the Parthenon. It's an amazing building, about 2,500 years old, and I'm sure the view from there (4) **will / is going to** be wonderful, too.

Later on, I think I (5) **'m going to / 'll go** shopping, and for the evening we've arranged something special. We (6) **'re having / 'll have** dinner by the sea, followed by music and dancing!

Tomorrow we (7) **'ll have to / 're having** to get up early, because we (8) **'re going / 'll go** to Corinth, along the coast. The train (9) **will leave / leaves** at 8.15, so I think we (10) **'ll have / 're having** plenty of time to go out to the site of Ancient Corinth.

Well, that's all for now. I (11) **'m posting / 'll post** this as soon as we go out and I hope it (12) **reaches / 's going to reach** you soon!

Love,

Jessica

Writing Part 1

Here are some sentences about a holiday.
For each question, complete the second sentence so that it means the same as the first. Use no more than three words.

Example:
Our holidays begin next week.
We're going ....*on holiday*............... next week.

1 It's a 15-minute car journey from the village to the coast.
   It takes 15 .... car from the village to the coast.

2 We'll stay in the car until we reach the end of the road.
   When we reach the end of the road, we'll get .... the car.

3 Then we'll walk to the beach.
   Then we'll .... foot to the beach.

4 At this time of year, the water is usually too cold to swim in.
   The water isn't .... to swim in at this time of year.

5 We'll probably stay in the village until the end of April.
   We .... leave the village until the end of April.

Listening Part 2

Exam advice

Always choose one of the answers, even if you have to guess.
You don't lose marks for wrong answers, but you can't get a mark if you put nothing.

You will hear a woman called Charlotte talking to an interviewer about her work as a weather forecaster.
For each question, put a tick (✓) in the correct box.

1 How long has Charlotte been a TV
  weather forecaster?
  A two years ☐
  B three years ☐
  C five years ☐

2 What does Charlotte enjoy most
  about her job?
  A working on a ship out at sea ☐
  B giving people useful information ☐
  C meeting people such as farmers ☐

3 Who, according to Charlotte, sometimes
  cancel their journey because of the forecast?
  A car drivers ☐
  B rail passengers ☐
  C aeroplane pilots ☐

4 Charlotte says that nowadays the television forecast is
  A never correct about the next seven
  days' weather. ☐
  B always correct about the next day's weather. ☐
  C usually correct about the next three
  days' weather. ☐

5 Charlotte says the use of modern technology
  A has its advantages and disadvantages. ☐
  B means she is on TV much more often. ☐
  C makes the forecaster's job simpler. ☐

6 Charlotte says that most people she meets
  A never watch the weather forecast on television. ☐
  B think that the weather forecast is always
  wrong. ☐
  C understand how difficult it is to forecast
  the weather. ☐

Vocabulary

Transport and weather

extremely, fairly, quite, rather, really, very

❶ **Look at the thermometer and fill in the gaps with *fairly, really, rather,***
  ***quite* or *extremely*.**

40+	.... hot	.... hot	
30–40	.... hot	.... hot	.... hot
20–30	warm		
10–20	cool		

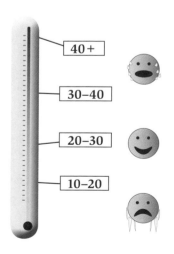

2 Write the words in the box next to the pictures and complete the table with prepositions.

plane   bus   bike   foot   car   train

1 get *on/onto*	get *off*	go *by*	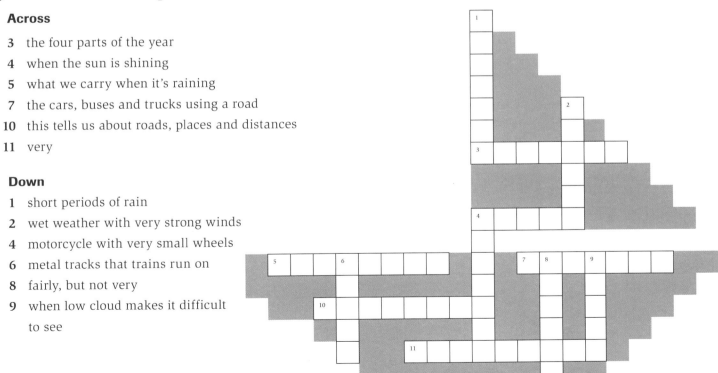	*bus*
2 get	get	go		
3 get	get	go		
4 get	get	go		
5 get	get	go		
6		go		

3 Read the clues and complete the crossword.

Across

3 the four parts of the year
4 when the sun is shining
5 what we carry when it's raining
7 the cars, buses and trucks using a road
10 this tells us about roads, places and distances
11 very

Down

1 short periods of rain
2 wet weather with very strong winds
4 motorcycle with very small wheels
6 metal tracks that trains run on
8 fairly, but not very
9 when low cloud makes it difficult
    to see

Unit 8 This is me!

Vocabulary

1 Look at the family tree and complete the sentences using a word in the box. There are two extra words you do not need to use.

| brother-in-law | nieces | twins | uncle | aunt | nephews | sister |
| father-in-law | grandchildren | granddaughter | sons | sister-in-law |

1 Lucy is Christine's ....
2 Simon is Sophie's ....
3 Tom and Ben are ....
4 Ben, Tom and Sam don't have a ....
5 Sophie is Lucy's ....
6 Ivor is Tim's ....
7 Tim is Lucy's ....
8 Sophie and Tim have three ....
9 Christine and Ivor have four ....
10 Katie and Simon have three ....

Christine and Ivor

Tim

Sophie

Katie

Simon

Sam

Ben and Tom

Lucy

2 Complete the sentences with the correct form of the phrasal verbs in the box.

| make up | look after | set up | get on with |
| grow up | bring up | find out | take up |

1 I don't .... my brother. We argue about everything.
2 My grandfather has .... playing tennis at the age of 70!
3 My uncle is very rich. He .... his own business twenty years ago.
4 When my mum was at work my aunt used to .... me.
5 For my grandmother's 60th birthday we are organising a surprise party. We don't want her to .... about it.
6 My sister always .... stories when she was little and now she wants to be a writer.
7 My cousin was born in London but she didn't .... there. She lived in New York until she was fifteen.
8 My dad wasn't .... by his parents. He lived with his grandparents from the age of five.

Reading Part 3

Exam advice

Remember the sentences follow the order of the text.

Look at the sentences below about two TV programmes.
Read the text below to decide if each sentence is correct or incorrect.
If it is correct, mark A in the box next to each statement.
If it is not correct, mark B in the box next to each statement.

		A	B
1	This is the first series of *Brat Camp*.	☐	☐
2	The aim of the series is to help mothers and daughters to get on better.	☐	☐
3	Mothers and daughters are dealt with kindly at the camp.	☐	☐
4	Each programme in the series shows the progress all the mothers and daughters are making.	☐	☐
5	It is possible to receive a copy of *The Anatomy of Peace* for free.	☐	☐
6	In *The World's Strictest Parents*, the teenagers are all from the same country.	☐	☐
7	The programme wants to prove that being strict is the best way to be a parent.	☐	☐
8	The teenagers stay with more than one host family.	☐	☐
9	The teenagers attend school while they are staying with the family.	☐	☐
10	During their stay with the host families, the teenagers learn why having rules is important.	☐	☐

TV Reviews

Brat Camp

Brat Camp returns as a brand new group of teenage girls, who are having problems at home, experience life in a camp in the Arizona desert. In this series, their mothers come with them to try to mend their broken relationships with their daughters.

Both mother and daughter receive a form of therapy called Anasazi, an approach that uses peace, love and understanding rather than strict rules and hard work.

Each week the programme concentrates on just one family, following their story from the moment they leave the UK to the time they return.

Will Anasazi's focus on spiritual health and independence have a positive effect? Can Dr Fred Dodini change the parenting habits of these desperate mothers and the behaviour of their difficult teenage daughters? Watch and find out.

The Arbinger Institute, whose philosophy and material are used as the basis of the Anasazi programme shown in 'Brat Camp', run free events. Their best-selling book, 'The Anatomy of Peace', tells the story of a family at the camp in Arizona.

The World's Strictest Parents

The World's Strictest Parents sends British teenagers to different countries around the world to live with strict families. This is an experiment to see if being strict is the right way to bring up a child and to find out whether strict parenting can change the relationship that problem teenagers have with their own parents.

The teenagers, aged between sixteen and nineteen, spend up to two weeks experiencing life with a family from a totally different culture. They can be sent anywhere from Jamaica to Jaipur and are expected to live under the strict rules of their host family, exactly as if they were the family's own child, and do as the host family's children do, both at school and at home.

Getting these teenagers to respect the rules isn't easy. But time away from home gives the teenagers an opportunity to compare their way of life and to see the value of having some order and discipline in their lives. From culture shock to self-discovery, these teenagers experience for the first time what it's like to live with strict parents – and to understand the benefits.

Grammar

Conditionals

❶ Match the two parts of the conditional sentences.

1	If my brother studied harder at school,	**a**	Luke won't talk to her any more.
2	If you didn't live so far away,	**b**	she'll phone you straightaway.
3	If Oliver didn't have to visit his aunt on Saturday,	**c**	Dad wouldn't get so angry with him.
4	Unless Hannah says she's sorry,	**d**	he'd play in the football match.
5	When Joe gives Ruby the message,	**e**	I won't be able to get a car.
6	If Lizzy wasn't always so rude,	**f**	we would see each other more often.
7	Unless my dad lends me the money,	**g**	you only have to ask.
8	If you want me to help you,	**h**	I'd invite her to my party.

❷ Circle the correct form of the verb.

1 Unless you *feel / felt* better, we *will / won't* go out tonight.

2 If I *am / were* more confident, I *enjoy / would enjoy* acting more.

3 When my brother *grows / grew* up, *he'll / he'd* be a famous footballer.

4 If you *get / got* the tickets after school, *I'd / I'll* give you the money tomorrow. Is that OK?

5 Now we live in the city but if we *live / lived* in the country, *I'd / I'll* have a tennis court in my garden.

6 Unless it *stops / stopped* raining, *we'll / we'd* have to cancel the picnic.

7 If I *had / would have* more time, *I'll / I'd* take up the guitar again but at the moment I've got to study for my exams.

8 When I *have / will have* a problem with my friends, my mum *helps / would help* me to sort it out.

❸ Complete the sentences so they are true for you.

1 If I lived in the city/country, I ....
....

2 If I had more time, ...
....

3 If I have a problem, ...
....

4 When I'm older, ...
....

5 If it rains at the weekend, ...
....

6 Unless I work hard, ...
....

Listening Part 3

Exam advice
Don't write long answers – one word or a short phrase is enough.

You will hear a head teacher giving some information to her students.
For each question, fill in the missing information in the numbered space.

Summer Programme: Firefighting skills for girls

Where: *Fire Training Centre*

Starts on: (1) ....

Number of students in group: 24

Students must be over (2) ....

Need students who are (3) .... and physically fit.

Students will benefit by becoming more (4) ....

Students only have to pay for (5) ....

For more information call Elaine (6) .... on 099898765.

Writing Part 2

Exam advice
Always check your spelling and punctuation. You will get a better mark if there aren't many mistakes.

❶ Look at the exam task and the student's answer below. Find SIX punctuation mistakes and FOUR spelling mistakes in Ricardo's email.

You recently went to your aunt's wedding but your English cousin wasn't able to go.
Write an email to your cousin. In your email you should:

- say what you enjoyed about the wedding
- describe your aunt's new husband
- ask your cousin's opinion of the photos you have sent.
  Write **35–45 words.**

Dear Fred

The wedding was good becaus it was in a beautifull hotel near the beach. the food was exelent. Aunt Emilias husband is quiet handsome but a little, bit bald! What do you think of these photos. I look the best, dont i?!

Take care

Ricardo

---

❷ Your English cousin recently got married but you couldn't go to the wedding. Write an email to your cousin. In your email you should:

- ask her about the wedding
- say why you couldn't go
- say when you will see her again.
  Write **35–45 words.**

Now check:

- you have included all three points. ☐
- your email is the right length. ☐
- your spelling. ☐
- your punctuation. ☐
- your grammar. ☐

Unit 9　Fit and healthy

Listening Part 4

Look at the six sentences for this part.
You will hear a conversation between Mike, a tennis coach, and Abbie, a girl who wants to learn to play tennis.
Decide if each sentence is correct or incorrect.
If it is correct, put a tick (✓) in the box under A for YES. If it is not correct, put a tick (✓) in the box under B for NO.

		A YES	B NO
1	Mike says that Abbie already holds the racket properly.	☐	☐
2	Mike thinks Abbie should watch tennis on television.	☐	☐
3	Abbie believes she is fit enough to be a top player.	☐	☐
4	Mike advises Abbie to start taking part in competitions now.	☐	☐
5	Abbie and Mike agree she needs to study the rules of tennis.	☐	☐
6	Abbie promises to do some exercise every day of the week.	☐	☐

Grammar

Relative clauses

❶ Match the sentence halves.

1	Basketball is a sport	a	who earn a huge amount of money.
2	Our team plays in that stadium,	b	whose sister is also a cylist, won her race.
3	Rafael Nadal is a tennis player	c	where many great runners live and train.
4	The Olympic Games of 1996,	d	which I really enjoy playing.
5	There are some footballers	e	who plays rugby, has broken his arm.
6	My elder brother, Jason,	f	whose name is known around the world.
7	My best friend, Olivia,	g	which was built a few years ago.
8	East Africa is the place	h	when I was born, were in Atlanta, USA.

② ⓐ Circle the correct relative pronouns.

1 I know a woman *which / who / whose* has sailed around the world.

2 Squash is a very fast sport *that / who / what* is played by two people.

3 One climber, *who / that / which* is now in hospital, fell ten metres.

4 My friend Mickey has a pair of skis *when / whose / which* he never uses.

5 The lake in the mountains, *where / which / that* we went swimming, was very cold.

6 People *who / whose / which* team always lose often seem miserable.

7 Let's go dancing on Saturday, *which / when / that* I'll have more time.

8 Table tennis, *that / which / when* is very popular in China, can be exciting to watch.

9 August is the month *which / when / where* we all go windsurfing in Tarifa, Spain.

10 One driver, *who / whose / that* car had broken down, was standing by the road.

11 Those are the hills *which / where / that* they have the mountain-biking races.

12 Professional athletes are people *that / which / whose* have to train every day.

ⓑ Which of sentences 1–12 would be correct without a relative pronoun?

Reading Part 5

Read the text below and choose the correct word for each space.
For each question, mark the correct letter A, B, C or D.

Example:

0 A before   **B** until   **C** since   **D** after

Answer:

0	A	B	C	D
	—	**—**	—	—

Our lives in numbers

From the day we are born (0) .... we reach old age, our bodies are changing and developing. Scientists now have more information than (1) .... before about these changes, and the facts and figures (2) .... us a lot about our lives.

In this country, the (3) .... person will live about eighty years. During that time, someone (4) .... health is generally good will walk 24,000 kilometres and sleep (5) .... 25 years. They will (6) .... three and a half years eating food that includes 1,200 chickens and 5,000 apples.

Some parts of the body keep (7) .... growing throughout our life. Each of our fingernails, for instance, grows about 3.5 centimetres every year, (8) .... means that during our life we grow 28 metres of nails.

Our hair, of course, gets longer much faster. Each one on our head grows 15 centimetres (9) .... year. So (10) .... of us will grow an amazing total of 950 kilometres of hair!

1	**A** then	**B** never	**C** ever	**D** soon
2	**A** tell	**B** inform	**C** say	**D** report
3	**A** usual	**B** medium	**C** standard	**D** average
4	**A** who	**B** whose	**C** where	**D** when
5	**A** for	**B** during	**C** while	**D** by
6	**A** use	**B** spend	**C** give	**D** pay
7	**A** at	**B** in	**C** on	**D** to
8	**A** that	**B** what	**C** which	**D** why
9	**A** a	**B** any	**C** the	**D** some
10	**A** much	**B** majority	**C** most	**D** lot

Vocabulary

Health and sport

❶ Complete the text with these nouns.

energy	breath	competition	injury
bat	treatment	court	net

Last year, my school organised a table-tennis
(1) .... for all fourth-year
students. I'd never played on a proper table-tennis
(2) .... before, or against such good
players. My first match was against Emilio Ramos, who
used a special (3) .... to hit the ball
really hard. It came over the (4) .... so
fast that I hardly saw it. I never stopped running and
jumping, and soon I was out of (5) ....
and had very little (6) .... left. I was
sure that Emilio would easily beat me, but then,
suddenly, he stopped. He had an (7) ....
to his left ankle, and he needed (8) ....
from the school nurse. I'd won!

❷ Read the clues and complete the crossword.

Across

1   something that shows you are not well
2   strong and in good health
5   sound that comes from your throat
7   common illness which is not very serious
8   blue or black mark on your skin
12   person who is not well
14   small, round piece of medicine that you swallow
15   illness caused by infection

Down

1   not feeling well
3   not in good health
4   pain, particularly in your head, ear or stomach
6   cause pain to part of your body, or to another person
9   painful
10   in good health
11   damage part of your body
12   another word for 14 across
13   person who takes care of people in hospital

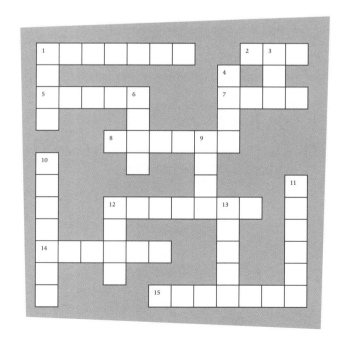

Writing Part 3 (story)

Exam advice

If you decide to write a story, make sure your text fits the title or the sentence you are given. Never change the title or this sentence in any way.

① Study the exam task and answer questions 1–4.

Your English teacher has asked you to write a story. This is the title for your story: *The missing case*.

1 What are the key words in the instructions?
2 Who will read your story?
3 Which words do you have to use? Where do they go?
4 Do you have to write the story in the first person (I), or the third person (he/she/it), or can you choose which you prefer?

② *(•)* **Read the story written by a PET candidate. Find and correct these three mistakes:**

- an incorrect verb form
- a relative pronoun
- a preposition of place.

③ Answer these questions about the story.

1 Is it about the right length?
2 Is it well organised into paragraphs?
3 Does the content of the story fit the title?
4 Which linking words, e.g. *because, before, so*, does the writer use?
5 Does the writer use a good variety of structures and verb tenses?
6 Is there a good range of vocabulary?
7 What kind of ending does the story have?

④ Now write your own story, following the exam instructions in 1.

Check your writing:

Is it the right length?   Yes/No

Are there paragraphs?   Yes/No

What linking words did you use? ....

....

Which tenses did you use? ....

....

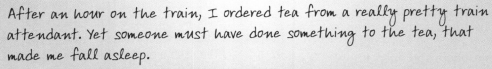

The missing case

It was like in a movie, exactly like in a movie. I always thought that something like that could never happen to me, but it did.

My boss, a really angry person, wanted me to take a small case to one of his clients in another city, so I was given a ticket for the next train there. If I had known what the case had been containing, I would have been more cautious ...

After an hour on the train, I ordered tea from a really pretty train attendant. Yet someone must have done something to the tea, that made me fall asleep.

When I woke up hours later, I realised that something was missing ... The case wasn't at its place any more! How would my boss react?

Reading Part 2

The people below all want to go to a restaurant for a celebration.
Decide which restaurant would be the most suitable for each person.

1  Stella wants to book a special family meal for her grandmother's 80th birthday. There will be a mix of ages so the menu needs to provide for a wide range of tastes. Stella's grandmother finds it difficult to hear so she doesn't want to take her anywhere which has loud music.

2  Elizabeth wants to book somewhere to celebrate her daughter's 18th birthday. She wants to invite about 20 family members and close friends. She is looking for somewhere special that can offer a reasonably priced dinner. She'd like the atmosphere to be friendly and informal.

3  Patrick wants to celebrate his first wedding anniversary. He wants to go to a first-class restaurant and doesn't mind how much it costs. He'd like somewhere that attracts famous people and for which his wife can put on her best dress.

4  Sadie wants to book a restaurant to celebrate the end of exams with a group of six friends. They don't want to spend much money but want to go somewhere with a lively atmosphere and interesting food.

5  Keith wants to celebrate his son Danny's birthday by taking him to try some top-quality cooking by a well-known chef. Danny is studying restaurant management at college and wants to run his own high-class restaurant one day.

RESTAURANTS

A *Max's Café* is a favourite venue with the stars for its amazing views across the river and excellent service, so you might find yourself on a table next to a well-known actor or politician. Prices are high but the perfectly-cooked, if slightly old-fashioned, food won't disappoint. Men must wear jackets and ties.

B One of the cheapest pizza and pasta restaurants in town, *JoJo's* remains very popular with groups of students for its live music and reasonable prices. The menu hasn't changed in 20 years but when it comes to food, *JoJo's* customers are more interested in value for money than excitement.

C Winner of the award for best service, *Justin's* is now offering a special menu for only £15 per person, giving people the chance to eat unusual food at affordable prices. The restaurant is always very busy and there's limited space for large groups. The staff are young and welcoming, although they are often in a hurry.

D Relax in comfort at the Regent Hotel's new *Terrace Restaurant*, while a classical pianist plays softly in the background. Tables are well spaced, so customers can hold their conversations in private. The menu, although certainly not cheap and a little on the dull side, is varied and there's something to please everyone.

E *Sammy's* is an excellent choice for those planning an event for a large group. Angela Hastings, former chef at the four-star *Pink* restaurant, specialises in good-quality simple food which is good value for money. Their aim is to please every type of customer. The staff make you feel very welcome. Live jazz most nights.

F This is a wonderful way to celebrate. Take a riverboat cruise and see the sights of the city as you eat. The menu is limited but not over-priced and the service is very professional. Most of the guests seem to be middle-aged couples. It can be cold so make sure you dress warmly.

G TV chef, Eliot Harris, has just opened his first restaurant, *Bitter Sweet*. Harris skilfully offers a mix of exciting and unusual ingredients, which those expecting more traditional food may find strange or even disgusting. A truly memorable experience for real food lovers. Book well in advance and expect to pay top of the range prices.

H *Grace's* is a magnificent venue, perfect for special occasions such as weddings. The dining room with its large balcony can be rented privately and can sit up to one hundred guests with plenty of space for dancing. The buffet menu is varied and very good value.

Grammar

❶ Put the words in the correct order and answer the questions.

1 you / cut / hair / your / have / do / ?

How often ....

....

2 teeth / did / checked / your / you / last / have / ?

When ....

....

3 have / you / photo / taken / your / do / ?

How often ....

....

4 last / eyes / have / did / you / your / tested / ?

When ....

....

5 get / you / do / replaced / mobile phone / your / ?

How often ....

....

6 have / bedroom / painted / last / did / your / you / ?

When ....

....

7 last / get / you / your / fixed / computer / did / ?

When ....

....

8 do / get / passport / changed / you / your / ?

How often ....

....

❷ Put the verbs in the present simple, present continuous or past simple form.

1 Mark .... (get) his car washed weekly.

2 Polly .... (have) her car repaired now.

3 Mum .... (have) a special cake made for my last birthday.

4 Joshua .... (get) his suits cleaned at the dry cleaner's once a month.

5 We .... (have) our new TV delivered last Saturday.

6 He .... (have) his computer fixed at the moment.

7 Isabelle and Vicky .... (get) new dresses specially made for their sister's wedding next May.

8 Our family .... (have) our photo taken for the local newspaper last week.

Vocabulary

Match the signs to the places.

1 Dry cleaner's ....   5 Dentist's ....

2 Garage ....   6 Library ....

3 Hairdresser's ....   7 Butcher's ....

4 Post office ....   8 Travel agent ....

A 20% discount this month on all bottles of shampoo

B Fines for the late return of all items will go up on April 1.

C It may not be possible to remove stains from silk ties.

D Please check if you need a visa for your chosen destination.

E Home-made award-winning sausages sold here.

F Please ask about our fast delivery service for small parcels (under 1kg).

G We recommend patients make regular appointments.

H Please make sure you have your tyres checked regularly.

Listening Part 1

Exam advice

Don't choose your answer before the end of the conversation. You may miss some important information. Then check your answer carefully during the second listening.

For each question there are three pictures and a short recording.
Choose the correct picture and put a tick (✓) in the box below it.

Example: What did the boy use to wear to school?

A ☐   B ☐   C ✓

1 What does the woman need?

 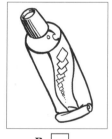 

A ☐   B ☐   C ☐

2 What time is the girl's appointment?

A ☐   B ☐   C ☐

3 What did the man have to eat in the restaurant?

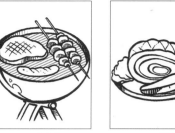 

A ☐   B ☐   C ☐

4 What kind of fruit does the girl decide to buy?

  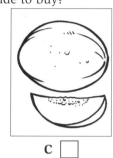

A ☐   B ☐   C ☐

5 What has the man had done?

A ☐   B ☐   C ☐

6 What is the woman complaining about?

A ☐   B ☐   C ☐

7 What does the boy want to borrow?

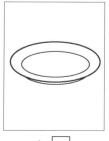  

A ☐   B ☐   C ☐

Writing Part 2

❶ Read the exam task and then the examples of students' writing. Tick the correct sentences.

You receive a postcard from an English-speaking friend, called Tom, telling you about the bad experience he had on holiday at a pizza restaurant you recommended.

Write a note to leave in Tom's locker. In your note you should

• apologise for recommending the restaurant

• explain why you think the restaurant has changed

• invite him to another pizza restaurant.

Write **35–40 words**.

Examples of students writing

Apologising

a I'm sorry about you had a bad experience at the restaurant. ☐

b I'm sorry to recommend the pizza restaurant. ☐

c I'm sorry for recommending the pizza restaurant. ☐

d I apologise for recommending the pizza restaurant. ☐

e Apologies for recommending the pizza restaurant. ☐

Explaining

f I explain you what I think happened. ☐

g I think there must be a new chef at the pizza restaurant. ☐

h The only explanation I can think of is that the cook was ill. ☐

Inviting

i I would to invite you to dinner. ☐

j I want to invite to another restaurant. ☐

k I'd like to invite you to another restaurant. ☐

l I will you invite to another restaurant. ☐

❷ Now you write the note to Tom.

❸ Check your work using the checklist.

Have you included all three points? ☐

Have you opened and closed the note correctly? ☐

Have you written 35–45 words? ☐

Are your spelling and punctuation correct? ☐

❹ (•) Read the task and the two students' notes. Answer the questions below with *A*, *B* or *Both*.

Your English friend Sam is coming to visit you and he wants to go with you to your favourite restaurant. Write a note to Sam. In your note you should

• say which restaurant you prefer

• describe the type of food

• suggest when you can go there together.

Note A

Dear Sam
My favourite restaurant is called "ROUTE 36". I like going here because the food is great. I love eating his desserts, specially his ice cream also it has a wonderful video games room. Do you fancy eating at the restaurant together?
See you soon
Stefano

Note B

Dear Sam
My favourit restaurant is called 'Rosa's Kitchen.' the food is exellent. You can ask for all type of food, pasta, or pizza and sandwiches. I always have spagettis, they are great. I hope you to answer me soon so we can go there together.
Martha

Which note ...

1 includes all three points? ....

2 is about the right length? ....

3 is ended well? ....

4 contains spelling mistakes? ....

5 contains punctuation mistakes? ....

6 contains grammar mistakes? ....

7 uses more food vocabulary? ....

Unit 11 Conserving nature

Reading Part 4

Exam advice
Remember that the middle three questions follow the order of the points in the text, but the first question and the last question are usually about the whole text.

Read what Claire did and the questions below. For each question, choose the correct answer A, B, C or D.

My stay in the rainforest

Last year, I left my job and went to Borneo to work without pay in the rainforest. So many people have said to me, 'I would love to do something like that,' and I say, 'If you want to, just do it.' They always reply, 'I can't.' But, if you really want to do it, there are ways to make it happen.

After three days' training, I started work on an environmental project with a group of young people. The accommodation was very basic and we had to build our own place to sleep. This consisted of a simple bed, a cloth roof and a net to keep insects out.

It was never dangerous there, but it was very challenging. There were things that we didn't think we would manage to do, but we did. I had some of my worst moments there, but also some of my best – it made me feel alive. I didn't miss my home comforts as much as I'd thought I might. We had food, water, somewhere to stay, about three sets of clothes and really good conversation. We were in the most beautiful place and we had things to keep us busy. We didn't need any more.

One of the teenagers said: 'Before we came here, it was really important to me what clothes I wore and who my friends were. I was always thinking about shoes, but really none of that matters. Here, people accept me for who I am, what I believe and think, not for what kind of clothes I've got.' When she said that, it summed it up for me.

1 What is the writer, Claire, trying to do in the text?
   A give the reader information about Borneo
   B advise people not to work in the Borneo rainforest
   C describe how she felt when she was in Borneo
   D explain what kind of work she did in Borneo

2 What does Claire tell other people?
   A Everyone must do the same as her.
   B Few people can do the same as her.
   C Nobody should do the same as her.
   D Anybody can do the same as her.

3 What does Claire say about her stay in the rainforest?
   A She had enough of everything that she needed.
   B She enjoyed having a comfortable room there.
   C She really missed some things from her home.
   D She knew she could deal with every problem.

4 How did Claire feel about living in the rainforest?
   A The experience had changed her attitudes.
   B She missed being with her friends at home.
   C It was difficult to make new friends there.
   D She was pleased everyone liked her clothes.

5 Which postcard did Claire write near the end of her stay in Borneo?

A
It's fantastic here! Nothing has gone wrong and everyone is really friendly. I don't think I ever want to go home.

B
I'm really enjoying myself here, despite a few difficulties. The scenery is wonderful, there's plenty to do and my colleagues are great.

Grammar

❶ Complete the text using the verbs in brackets. Use the present simple or the past simple in the passive.

Last year, some of us decided to investigate how much (1) ....was wasted........ (waste) at our school, and the answer was clear: far too much! Almost all paper, plastic, metal and glass (2) .... (throw out) with other rubbish, so very little material (3) .... (recycle). Empty drink cans and plastic bottles (4) .... (leave) on the floor next to the machines, and old books, magazines and papers (5) .... (mix) with other waste. We (6) .... (shock) by what we found, so a meeting with our teachers (7) .... (arrange). As a result, some big changes (8) .... (make) to the way the school deals with waste. Now students and staff (9) .... (ask) to put all cans and plastic containers into special bins next to the drinks machines, waste paper (10) .... (collect) from each classroom every week, and bottles (11) .... (separate) into three colours: green, brown and clear glass. There's still a lot to do, but we're pleased that nowadays so much of the waste material from our school (12) .... (use) again instead of being burnt or buried, which is so bad for the environment.

C

It's quite good here, although at first we didn't have enough to eat and drink. There's also a problem with insects, but I've put up a net now.

_____

_____

_____

_____

D

I'm missing my home more than I expected, but the people here are all very friendly. We chat a lot and we work together well.

_____

_____

_____

_____

❷ Here are some sentences about a visit to a safari park. For 1–10, complete the second sentence so that it means the same as the first. Use no more than three words, including a passive verb form.

1 Last week the school took us to a safari park.
   We .... to a safari park last week.

2 Before we arrived, the teacher said we had to be careful.
   We .... that we had to be careful before we arrived.

3 'You must stay on the bus all the time,' she said.
   'You are .... to get off the bus at any time,' she said.

4 When we got into the park they showed us the lions.
   We .... the lions when got into the park.

5 The staff in the park usually feed the lions every morning.
   The lions .... every morning by the staff.

6 But on that occasion somebody made a mistake.
   But a mistake .... on that occasion.

7 Six hungry lions suddenly approached our bus.
   Our bus .... by six hungry lions.

8 Fortunately, one of the staff saw the lions coming near us.
   Fortunately, the lions .... coming near us.

9 He quickly gave the hungry animals a huge meal.
   The hungry animals .... a huge meal.

10 'These lions never attack anybody!' he said, laughing.
    Laughing, he said 'Nobody .... by these lions!'

Listening Part 2

Exam advice
Not all of the information in the recording is tested, so you don't need to understand everything you hear. Concentrate on the points that <u>are</u> tested.

You will hear a man called Neil Curran talking about wildlife programmes on television.
For each question, put a tick (✓) in the correct box.

1 What time can you see *Wildlife on Three* today?
   A at 6 pm ☐
   B at 6.45 pm ☐
   C at 7.30 pm ☐

2 Tomorrow's programme on Indian wildlife is mainly about
   A unusual fish. ☐
   B insects and birds. ☐
   C large animals. ☐

3 *Desert Watch* describes plants that
   A get water from the air. ☐
   B die when it doesn't rain. ☐
   C grow close to rivers. ☐

4 What is the problem on the island?
   A There are few rabbits left. ☐
   B There aren't enough plants. ☐
   C Cats are attacking the birds. ☐

5 What is the plan for the coast?
   A to let the water partly cover the land ☐
   B to encourage birds to leave the area ☐
   C to prevent sea water flooding the land ☐

6 Why, according to Neil, are wildlife programmes so popular?
   A They always have a lot of variety. ☐
   B People of different ages can enjoy them. ☐
   C They are on quite early in the evening. ☐

Writing Part 3 (letter)

Exam advice
Always leave some time at the end to check your letter carefully for mistakes. Look particularly for any grammar, vocabulary, word order, spelling or punctuation errors.

❶ Study the exam task and answer questions 1–4.

This is part of a letter you receive from an English penfriend.

I've just come back from a really good holiday away from the city.
Where do you most like to spend your holidays? Do you think I would enjoy going there?

Now write a letter, answering your penfriend's questions. Write your letter in about 100 words.

1 What are the key words in the instructions?
2 Who do you have to write to?
3 What does this person tell you?
4 What does he or she want to know?

❷ (•) Find and correct twelve mistakes in this letter written by a PET candidate. For each one, write *verb form, preposition, word order, vocabulary, article, singular/plural* or *spelling*.

Hi Liz

Thanks very much for your letter. I'm really pleased that you had a great holiday in this year.

I always prefer spend my holidays in the countryside. I love nature! I choose usually a quiet place near the forest and next to lake. I enjoy walks in the countryside and I love beatiful scenery. I like swim in the lake and go into the forest.

I always go in my holidays with my friends. In the evenings we sit next to the fire and chat about different subject. We also make trips to the Nationale Park.

You must spend your holidays here! You fall in love with this country. I'm looking to forward hearing from you.

Love,

Jay

3 Answer these questions about the letter.

1 Is the length of the letter about right?

2 Is it well organised into paragraphs?

3 What does the writer say about Liz's news?

4 Does the writer answer both of her questions? In which paragraphs?

5 Is there a good range of grammar and vocabulary?

6 Which common letter-writing expressions are used at the beginning and end?

Vocabulary

The natural world

Read the clues and complete the crossword.

Across

3 animal with a tail that lives in 13 down

7 oil, petrol, coal, gas, wood, etc.

8 big animal sometimes hunted in forests

9 large reptile with sharp teeth

10 give food to an animal

12 animal that someone keeps at home

17 the biggest land animal on Earth

18 big fish with very sharp teeth

19 all plants, animals, materials, weather, etc.

20 large animal with black and white lines

Down

1 the Earth goes round this once a year

2 water that is frozen and solid

4 large animal that lives in Australia

5 animals, birds, fish, insects, plants, etc.

6 big, strong animal with thick hair

9 container with metal bars where animals
 are kept

11 big friendly animal that lives in the sea

12 energy, particularly from electricity

13 very tall plant with branches and leaves

14 large area with lots of 13 down

15 big, light brown wild cat

16 any animal, bird, fish or insect –
 but not a plant

What did you say?

Reading Part 4

Exam advice
Answer Q1 and 5 last when you have understood the text better. They test overall understanding.

Read the text and questions below.
For each question, mark the correct letter A, B, C or D.

Life Before the Mobile Phone

Once upon a time if we wanted to make a phone call or wait for someone to contact us, we had to sit at home or at our desks. There were public phones in the street of course, but it could be hard to find one that was working and there were often long queues to use them. And of course you had to remember to bring a lot of coins to pay for the calls. So people didn't phone their friends as often.

Mobile phones, or cellphones as the Americans call them, these small pieces of electronic equipment which allow us to talk with friends and family while we are on the move, have dramatically changed the way we live.

Before the age of the mobile phone, our loved ones would sit around worried sick if we were late coming home. There were no quick calls to tell mum that there would be additional guests coming for dinner. We would have to depend on notes left on fridges or desks to communicate messages. How did we survive?

But mobile phones have also had a negative effect and what people don't seem to realise is that we've lost something very valuable: our privacy. Now our friends and family can contact us wherever and whenever they want to. We can never get away from them.

The way people communicate with each other is completely different now. It's difficult to have a conversation face-to-face with a friend without being interrupted every couple of minutes by the ring of their phone. Most people don't see anything wrong in having a long conversation on their mobile phone while forgetting all about the person sitting opposite they are supposed to be talking to. It seems the art of real conversation may be dying.

Of course, people could leave their mobile phones at home or even switch them off but no one ever does that. Why not? Because the worrying thing is we can't live without our phones. We've become communication addicts, unable to spend even a few minutes out of contact, in case we miss something 'important'.

1 What is the writer's main purpose in writing this article?
   A to inform people about methods of communication in the past
   B to show the disadvantages of the way people communicate today
   C to persuade people to stop using mobile phones
   D to compare different types of phone conversations

2 What point does the writer make about using telephones before the invention of mobile phones?
   A Using a telephone was very expensive.
   B Phone calls were much shorter.
   C People made fewer phone calls.
   D People were more dependent on public telephones.

3 What does the writer think about life before mobile phones?
   A It was more inconvenient.
   B People were more punctual.
   C Things were more relaxed.
   D Everyone managed very well.

4 What is the writer's main argument against mobile phones?
   A They have damaged relationships.
   B It's impossible to escape from them.
   C They are bad for our health.
   D We give out too much personal information.

5 Which word best describes how the writer feels about the use of mobile phones?
   A angry
   B excited
   C anxious
   D surprised

Grammar
Reported speech and reported commands

❶ Complete the sentences in reported speech.

1 'I don't know the answer.'
  He said .... the answer.

2 'Dad is going to take you to the station today.'
  Mum said Dad .... that day.

3 'We've never been to Australia.'
  They said .... to Australia.

4 'I'm sorry that I didn't do my homework.'
  She said she .... homework.

5 'Tom will phone you tomorrow.'
  She said .... the next day.

6 'Maria and Jane finished university last year.'
  He said .... the year before.

7 'I can't remember where I bought my watch.'
  Granddad said .... watch.

8 'My laptop is broken, so I can't send any emails.'
  She said .... any emails.

❷ Look at the reported commands and write the instructions.

Example
  The teacher told them to write an essay for homework.
  'Write an essay for homework.'

1 Her mum told her to go to bed.
  ....

2 She told him to phone as soon as he arrived.
  ....

3 Ellie's brother told her not to use his iPod.
  ....

4 My teacher told us not to worry about the exam.
  ....

5 We told them not to eat all the chocolate.
  ....

❸ Cristina has just done her PET Speaking Test. She tells Marta about the questions her partner asked her during a discussion about radio in Part 4. Write what Cristina says to Marta.

1 **Partner:** How often do you listen to the radio?
My partner asked me how

....

to the radio.

2 **Partner:** Do you prefer listening to the radio or to music on your iPod?
My partner asked me

....

3 **Partner:** Where and when do you listen to the radio?
My partner asked me

....

4 **Partner:** What is the most popular radio station in your town?
My partner asked me

....

Listening Part 3

Exam advice
Read through the information before you listen and think about the kind of words you need to fill the gaps.

You will hear a radio presenter giving some information about a new exhibition.
For each question, fill in the missing information in the numbered spaces.

Pirate Radio Exhibition

History of Radio Caroline:

• based on a radio ship

• started in (1) ....

Exhibition includes:

• original records and (2) .... from music fans

• interviews with (3) .... from Radio Caroline

Visitor information:

• opening times: (4) ....

• exhibition will close in (5) ....

Ticket information: (6) .... entrance.

Vocabulary

Complete the signs with the correct preposition of location. Sometimes more than one answer is possible.

1  Please do not park

.... these gates.

2  Please wait

.... the line.

3  Danger! Do not walk

.... the bridge.

4  New burger restaurant!

.... the cinema.

5  Please stand

....

6  Remember to drive

.... !

7 Do not take photographs

.... the museum.

8 Please ski

.... the flags.

Writing Part 3

Exam advice
Read the instructions carefully. If the question tells you to begin with the sentence given, do NOT change this sentence in any way.

1 **Look at the task and two students' stories on the right.**

You have to write a story for your English teacher. Your story must begin with this sentence:

I was really surprised when I read the email.

Write your story in **about 100 words.**

Now answer the questions below. Tick one or both boxes for each question.

Which story	Story A	Story B
1 has a clear ending?	☐	☐
2 is easy to understand?	☐	☐
3 makes mistakes with reported speech?	☐	☐
4 contains punctuation errors?	☐	☐
5 contains a spelling error?	☐	☐
6 repeats the same linking word(s) several times?	☐	☐
7 has the right number of words?	☐	☐

2 **Correct the errors in the stories.**

3 **Write your own story beginning with the sentence**

'I was really surprised when I read the email.'

Write about 100 words. Remember to check your work carefully.

Story A

I was really surprised when I read the email. In the first line I couldn't believe that it was the truth, but it was, I won a prize of about ten thousand american dollars, but there was a problem I needed to go personally to get the prize, but it was the same date of my final exam of physics! I didn't know what could I do. I spoke with my parents and they tell me that it is my decicion. I spoke with my teacher and he said I can take the exam next week. I was really happy that I got my prize.

Story B

I was really surprised when I read the email. I thought Ana was still angry with me. Last year our mothers didn't let us go to a party. So I had an idea. I said my mother I was sleeping at Ana's house and she said hers she was sleeping at my house. So, we went to the party. We really had a good time. But the next day my mother told me that Ana's mother had phoned and asked if Ana was at my house. So our mothers found out the truth. Ana's mother didn't let her go to a party for a whole year. Ana said it was my fault and that she would never speak to me again. But today in her email Ana said she wants to see me as soon as possible.

Unit 1   Vocabulary Extra

House and home

1 a Match the parts of the house with 1–12.

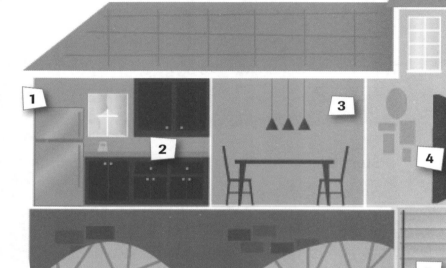

kitchen .... hall .... stairs .... wall ....
bathroom .... roof .... living room .... bedroom ....
ceiling .... lavatory .... chimney .... dining room ....

b Put these items into the correct column.
You can use your dictionary.

| shower | frying pan | duvet | alarm clock |
| kettle | hairdryer | freezer | sheets |

bedroom	bathroom	kitchen

c Add three more things you might see in each room.

2 a Put these nouns in two groups: countable and uncountable. Write the plural form of the countable nouns. You can use your dictionary.

rain   heating   windmill   furniture   dish
food   cave   shampoo   flat   switch
bin   make-up   plug   curtain   sunshine
housework   cottage   money   blind
cleaning   electricity   step   shelf
air-conditioning

Countable	Uncountable
windmill – windmills	rain

b Add three more nouns to each group.

Unit 2 Vocabulary Extra

Daily life

❶ Complete the past simple form of these irregular verbs.

1	eat	_ _ e	6	learn	l _ _ _ _ _
2	buy	b _ _ _ _ t	7	lose	l _ _ _
3	drive	d _ _ _ e	8	ring	r _ _ _
4	have	h _ _	9	spend	s _ _ _ _
5	leave	l _ _ _	10	take	t _ _ _

❷ Write the nouns under the correct verbs. Some of the nouns can go with more than one verb.

sport	breakfast	a break	a job	fun
homework	money	time		a suggestion
a wage	friends	a decision		

do	make	have	spend	earn

❸ Tick the things you do every day. Tick which things you didn't do yesterday. Write sentences.

	every day	yesterday
• Drive to school	☐	☐
• Buy a train/bus ticket	☐	☐
• Take the dog for a walk	☐	☐
• Learn some new English words	☐	☐
• Lose your mobile phone	☐	☐
• Ring for a taxi	☐	☐
• Leave the house early in the morning	☐	☐
• Spend a lot of time doing homework	☐	☐
• Eat a sandwich for lunch	☐	☐

Example: *I usually drive to school. I didn't buy a train ticket yesterday.*

❹ Match the functions A–D with the examples 1–8.

A apologising

B inviting

C suggesting

D explaining

1 Would you like to watch the football match at my house?

....

2 We could meet on Thursday after school.

....

3 I can't come to the cinema because I've got to finish my History essay.

....

4 I'm sorry I couldn't go to your party.

....

5 Let's ask Alfie if he wants to play football on Saturday.

....

6 The problem was I missed the bus. That's why I was late for school.

....

7 There's one ticket left for the concert if you'd like to come.

....

8 Why don't you tell your teacher about the problem?

....

Unit 3 Vocabulary Extra

Hobbies and free time

1 a Write the names of the activities next to pictures A–D.

A .... B .... C .... D ....

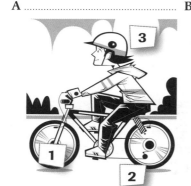   

b Match words a–l with 1–12 in the pictures, using your dictionary if you need to.

a guitar	**b** board	**c** keyboard	**d** wave
e wheel	**f** tyre	**g** tent	**h** wetsuit
i helmet	**j** backpack	**k** drums	**l** sleeping bag

2 Add negative prefixes to these adjectives and put them in the correct column. If you need to, you can use your dictionary.

fair	correct	complete	true	dependent
patient	fit	lucky	possible	kind
polite	perfect	formal	healthy	known
direct	probable	tidy		

un-	im-	in-
unfair		

3 Match sentences 1–8 with a–h, making sure they have similar meanings.

1 A neighbour **looks after** my cats when I'm away.

2 I **set out** at 6.30 am on Saturday.

3 I might **take up** a hobby.

4 I'm working hard to **catch up with** everyone else.

5 I won't **give up** attempting to break the record.

6 I don't **feel like** going out at the moment.

7 I **get off** at the last station.

8 I can **deal with** problems like this.

a I stay on the train all the way there.

b I'm doing all I can to reach the same level as the others.

c I'd prefer to stay in right now.

d I know what to do about this kind of situation.

e My journey begins early in the morning this weekend.

f When I'm not at home, somebody takes care of my pets for me.

g I think I'll start doing an activity in my spare time.

h I'm going to keep trying to do it better than anyone else.

Unit 4 Vocabulary Extra

Describing places

1 **Write the words.**
The first letter has been done for you.

1

buy s ....

2

go s ....

3

go s ....

4

go t ....

5

take p ....

6

go s ....

2 **Match the places 1–6 with the information A–F.**

1 youth club   **2** tourist office   **3** department store
4 town hall   **5** police station   **6** museum

A
Sale now on. All sports equipment half price.

B
Entrance free.
Please do not take photos.

C
Book your hotel or hostel here.

D
What do think about our local services? Public meeting here on Thursday.

E
Please dial the emergency number if we are closed.

F
Open from 8-10.00pm.
Everyone aged 15-17 welcome.

3 **Write the opposite adjective.**

1 He didn't catch a tiny fish.
He caught an .... fish!

2 He didn't dive into deep water.
He dived into .... water!

3 It wasn't freezing cold in the tent.
It was .... hot.

4 It wasn't flat where we went walking.
It was .... !

5 The atmosphere at the party wasn't lively.
It was .... !

6 It wasn't safe to swim in the sea.
It was .... !

4 **Circle the two adjectives that fit in each sentence.**

1 The restaurant was quite *modern / crowded / tiny*.

2 The internet café is really *expensive / big / deep*.

3 The shopping centre is absolutely
fantastic / old / terrible.

4 The river is very *filthy / dirty / narrow*.

5 The stadium is absolutely
modern / enormous / wonderful.

6 The market is extremely
interesting / fascinating / cheap.

7 The factory was quite *noisy / terrible / dangerous*.

8 The town is extremely *lively / great / nice*.

Unit 5   Vocabulary Extra

Feelings

1 a How do you feel? Complete the sentences with the adjectives. You can use your dictionary.

amused	curious	ashamed
nervous	pleased	impatient
lazy	confident	jealous upset

When you're feeling:

1 ...., you want something that someone else has.

2 ...., you're unhappy about something that's happened.

3 ...., you think something is funny.

4 ...., you want something to happen soon.

5 ...., you don't want to do any work.

6 ...., you want to know about something.

7 ...., you know you've done something bad.

8 ...., you're certain you can do something.

9 ...., you're worried about something that might happen.

10 ...., you're happy about something that's happened.

b Which of 1–10 in 1a do you think are positive emotions, which are negative, and which are neither positive nor negative? Put + or – next to the positive and negative adjectives.

2 Fill in the gaps with the correct preposition: *about*, *of* or *with*.

1 Some children are afraid .... the dark.

2 I'm sorry .... forgetting to phone you.

3 I was embarrassed .... my silly mistake.

4 Ben was satisfied .... the work he'd done.

5 Chloe is proud .... her daughter's success.

6 I'm angry .... Sam for telling me lies.

7 I was disappointed .... the food in that café.

8 We were sad .... leaving our old house.

9 Alex is frightened .... some insects.

10 I'm not sure .... the date of the wedding.

3 a Match the adjectives and their opposites. You can use your dictionary.

boring	mean	kind
intelligent	rude	cheerful

1 polite   ....

2 stupid   ....

3 generous   ....

4 cruel   ....

5 interesting   ....

6 miserable   ....

b For each pair of adjectives, which one is positive and which is negative? Put + or – next to each adjective.

Unit 6 Vocabulary Extra

TV and clothes

❶ Match the TV programmes 1–6 to the TV Guide A–F.

1 cartoon	2 documentary	3 comedy series
4 the news	5 quiz show	6 chat show

TV Guide

A 7.30
Final programme in the series; this time we learn about life under the sea.

B 2.45
More adventures with Lenny, the orange and blue striped lion.

C 5.15
Catch the latest information on the train drivers' strike.

D 8.30
An opportunity to meet star guest, Amy Ellison.

E 10.15
Jack gets a job in the circus and gets to know a snake. Painfully funny.

F 9.30
Will Ali answer all the questions and win the competition? Watch and find out.

❷ Write the word. The first letter has been written for you.

1

b ....

2

w ....

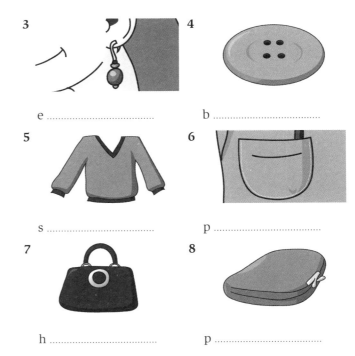

3

e ....

4

b ....

5

s ....

6

p ....

7

h ....

8

p ....

❸ Match the descriptions to the correct picture.

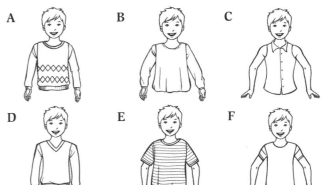

A   B   C

D   E   F

Max is wearing

1 a striped T-shirt with short sleeves.   ....
2 a T-shirt which is too tight.   ....
3 a T-shirt with long sleeves and a round neck...............
4 an old-fashioned patterned sweater.   ....
5 a sleeveless shirt.   ....
6 a cotton sweater with a V-neck.   ....

Unit 7   Vocabulary Extra

Weather and transport

❶ Complete compound words 1–10 and match them with pictures A–J.

roads	post	book	ground	way
about	hiker	pack	bike	case

A  B   C   D

E   F   G   H

I   J

1	suit	case	F
2	motor	....	....
3	sign	....	....
4	under	....	....
5	guide	....	....
6	cross	....	....
7	hitch	....	....
8	back	....	....
9	round	....	....
10	rail	....	....

❷ Complete the sentences using six of the compound words you formed in Exercise 1. Then write your own sentences containing the other four words.

1 Trains first ran on this .... 150 years ago.

2 Tourists use a .... to find a good hotel.

3 I carried everything in my .... so that my hands were free.

4 We stopped at the .... when the traffic lights turned red.

5 I tried to .... on the main road, but none of the cars stopped.

6 The .... on the country road said 'Newtown 8 miles'.

❸ Look at the weather symbols next to 1–8. Complete the descriptions with the correct form of the words in the box. You will need to use some of them more than once.

rain	sun	frost	thunder	degree	ice
lightning	cloud	snow	wind	temperature	

1 The .... is very high.
It's 45 .... centigrade.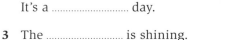

2 There are a lot of .... in the sky.
It's a .... day.

3 The .... is shining.
It's a .... day.

4 The .... is blowing strongly.
It's a very .... day.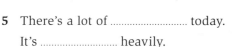

5 There's a lot of .... today.
It's .... heavily.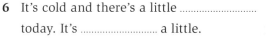

6 It's cold and there's a little ....
today. It's .... a little.

7 The sky's lit up by .... , then
there's the sound of ....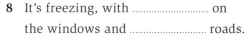

8 It's freezing, with .... on
the windows and .... roads.

Unit 8 Vocabulary Extra

Describing people

❶ Look at the family photo and complete the sentences with a word from the box.

broad	looks	moustache	thin	blonde
wavy	bald	straight	medium	fair
dark	scar	smart	curly	

Mr Spike is very tall and very (1) ....
He's almost completely (2) .... and he has
a long (3) .... He has a (4) ....
across his face. Mrs Spike has short (5) ....
(6) .... hair and is very pale. She is younger
than her husband. She only (7) .... about
35 years old. She's very attractive in a scary
sort of way and wears (8) .... clothes.
Luther Spike is quite good-looking. He's
(9) .... height with (10) ....
shoulders. He's got long (11) ....
(12) .... hair. His sister Eva is shorter
than him. She's (13) .... with long
(14) .... hair and is quite plain.

❷ Write the opposites. The first letter has been written for you.

1 lazy   h ....   2 stupid   s ....   3 quiet   n ....   4 generous   m ....

5 polite   r ....   6 nervous   c ....   7 shy   c ....   8 cold   w ....

❸ Choose one of the adjectives in the box (with or without a prefix) for descriptions 1–8.

childish	cheerful	(un)friendly	(im)patient	(un)reliable	(dis)honest	selfish

1 A person who likes meeting new people is ....

2 A person who laughs and smiles a lot is ....

3 A person who never arrives on time is ....

4 A person who only thinks about himself is ....

5 A person who steals things is ....

6 A person you can trust is ....

7 A person who gets annoyed easily if they have to wait is ....

8 A person who acts too young for their age is ....

Unit 9 Vocabulary Extra

Sport and health

1 ⓐ Match the places 1–6 with the names of the sports a–f.

1	pool	a	gymnastics
2	gym	b	swimming
3	pitch	c	boxing
4	track	d	athletics
5	ring	e	basketball
6	court	f	football

ⓑ Which sports a–f above do we *go, do* or *play*? Think of more sports that take each of these verbs, e.g. *go sailing*.

2 Match the words in the box with the pictures. Write down three sports that use each.

boots	helmet	trainers
gloves	shorts	racket

1 .... 2 .... 3 ....

....

....

4 .... 5 .... 6 ....

....

....

3 ⓐ Complete the table with the sports verbs.

verb	past simple	past participle
throw	threw	thrown
win		
lose		
draw		
beat		
score		
hit		
kick		

ⓑ Complete the sentences with the above verbs.

1 You ....score........ a goal or points in a game or match.
2 You .... a ball with a racket or bat.
3 You .... a game if you score more than the other player or team.
4 You .... a ball with your foot.
5 You .... another player or team if you score more than them.
6 You .... a game if you score less than the other player or team.
7 You .... a ball or other object with your hand.
8 You .... a game if you score the same as the other player or team.

4 Look at accidents and illnesses 1–8. Match them with treatments a–h.

1	deep wound	a	aspirin
2	possible fracture	b	medicine
3	extreme stress	c	operation
4	small cut	d	x-ray
5	broken leg	e	bandage
6	headache	f	plaster
7	sore throat	g	relaxation
8	sprained wrist	h	plaster cast

Unit 10 Vocabulary Extra

Food, house and home

❶ Find the words.

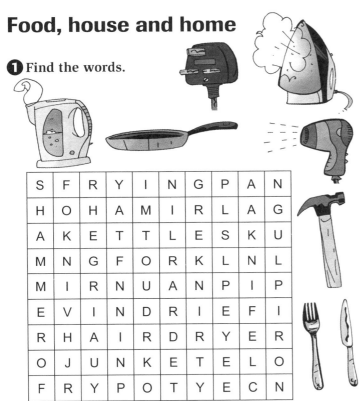

S	F	R	Y	I	N	G	P	A	N
H	O	H	A	M	I	R	L	A	G
A	K	E	T	T	L	E	S	K	U
M	N	G	F	O	R	K	L	N	L
M	I	R	N	U	A	N	P	I	P
E	V	I	N	D	R	I	E	F	I
R	H	A	I	R	D	R	Y	E	R
O	J	U	N	K	E	T	E	L	O
F	R	Y	P	O	T	Y	E	C	N

❷ Match the words and the definitions.

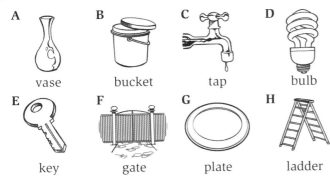

A vase   B bucket   C tap   D bulb

E key   F gate   G plate   H ladder

1 This is made of wood. It's usually kept closed so that cows and sheep in fields can't escape.

2 This is usually made of glass. It's used to put flowers in.

3 This is usually made of plastic. It's used to hold water in.

4 This is made of metal. You need it to unlock your front door.

5 This is made of glass and metal. You put it in lamps to provide light.

6 This can be made of glass, plastic or paper. You put your food on it.

7 This is made of wood or metal. You climb on it when you want to paint a ceiling.

8 This is made of metal. You turn it on when you want to wash your hands.

❸ Complete the shopping list with a noun of quantity.

slice   jar   bar   tube   loaf
carton   tin/can   bottle

2 .... of soap   a ....of bread
a .... of chocolate   a .... of milk
some .... of cheese   4 .... of water
a .... of honey   a .... of tomatoes
a .... of toothpaste

❹ Complete the sentences with a word from the box.

dish   meal   desserts
food   starter   vegetarian

1 Which type of .... do you prefer? Italian or Chinese?

2 In many countries breakfast is only a very small ....

3 My mum doesn't like making .... She always buys cakes and tarts from the supermarket.

4 If I'm having a three-course meal, I always choose soup as a ....

5 There's always a local .... on the menu at my dad's favourite restaurant.

6 I mainly eat .... food although I sometimes eat fish.

Unit 11   Vocabulary Extra

Environment and the natural world

1 Label the diagram with these words.

the Sun	a star	the Earth	a planet	the moon

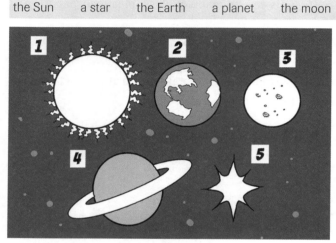

1 ....   2 ....   3 ....
4 ....   5 ....

2 Label the diagram with these words.

field	forest	hill	lake
mountain range		river	rock
sand	waterfall	wave	

1 ....   2 ....   3 ....
4 ....   5 ....   6 ....
7 ....   8 ....   9 ....
10 ....

3 Complete the expressions *in italics* with these words.

bottle	climate	light	public
rubbish	solar	tropical	wild

1   In the Arctic there are some fascinating .... *animals* such as polar bears.

2   The best way to travel in the city centre is by .... *transport*.

3   The sudden changes in the weather may be a result of .... *change*.

4   Our water is heated by .... *energy*.

5   The areas of .... *rainforest* in the world are getting smaller.

6   We always put our empty glass containers into the .... *bank*.

7   These new .... *bulbs* use much less electricity than the old ones.

8   That food isn't fresh. Put it in the .... *bin* now.

4 a Add the correct suffix, *-ation*, *-ion*, or *–ment*, to each group of nouns.

1   attract   connect   discuss
    protect   invent   collect   ....

2   advertise develop   disappoint
    enjoy   entertain excite
    improve   replace   ....

3   confirm   consider   form
    inform   relax   ....

b Add *-ation*, *-ion*, or *–ment* to these nouns, making the necessary spelling changes. You can use your dictionary.

admire	argue	celebrate
communicate	complete	conserve
create	describe	educate
examine	explain	invite
pollute	prepare	pronounce
register	reserve	translate

Unit 12 Vocabulary Extra

Social interaction and directions

❶ Complete the sentences with one of the words in the box.

speak	say	chat	slang
texts	communicate	tell	ask

1 Don't .... me what happens at the end of the film.
2 To .... well you need to listen carefully to what people are saying.
3 You shouldn't use .... in your English essays.
4 I .... online with my friends every day.
5 You should always .... what you think and be honest with people.
6 I send about twenty .... a day, which my dad thinks is too many.
7 I wonder if I can .... for her telephone number.
8 My mum can .... French and Spanish very well.

❷ Write the nouns with verbs they are often used with.

lies   plans   a joke
help   hello   information   the truth
a language   the answers   to friends
dreams   a story   goodbye

say	tell	speak	talk about	ask for

❸ Look at the picture and read the sentences. True (T) or false (F)?

Fred lives at number 10, Summer Road.

1 Fred's house is between the café and the bank. ....
2 From the café you have to walk past two buildings to get to the park. ....
3 There's a bus stop in front of Fred's house. ....
4 There's a large tree behind the bank. ....
5 Inside the café it's very crowded and there are people waiting outside. ....
6 The library is opposite the park. ....
7 Someone has left a bicycle on a balcony. ....
8 A cat has climbed on the roof of the bank. ....

Answer key

Unit 1
Reading Part 5

1 D **2** D **3** C **4** A **5** D **6** B **7** A **8** C **9** B **10** C

Grammar

❶ **2** watching → watch **3** shows → is/'s showing
4 stay → are/'re staying **5** wearing → wear
6 leave → am/'m leaving **7** I'm wearing →
I (usually) wear **8** look → are/'re looking
9 is speaking → speaks **10** send → am/'m sending

❷ **2** am/'m writing **3** am/'m staying **4** am/'m living
5 go **6** speak **7** understand **8** is/'s getting
9 need **10** like **11** don't want **12** remember

Listening Part 4

1 A **2** B **3** A **4** B **5** A

Recording script   CD1 Track 1

Leon: What do you think of my room, Zara? Don't you think it looks small? I haven't got much furniture, but it feels like there's very little space here.

Zara: Well, it's exactly the same size as my room and I'm quite happy there, but (1) <u>I see what you mean, Leon.</u> Your room just seems smaller than it really is, I think.

Leon: Why do you think that is?

Zara: The first thing, I think, is that it's too dark. The walls and the ceiling, I mean.

Leon: So would it be a good idea to paint everything white?

Zara: Well, that might make it look a bit like an office, or a hospital. (2) <u>Yellow or light green would be better, I think.</u> Then you could get things like cushions in the same colour, and perhaps do something about the colour of the furniture. Some of that's very dark, too.

Leon: Yes, and I could paint things like the cupboards myself. I noticed the other day that the supermarket is selling big tins of paint really cheaply, so I could start straightaway.

Zara: Hmm. I'm not sure about that. (3) <u>It's probably best to ask Mum and Dad what they think first.</u>

Leon: Oh, I don't think they'll mind.

Zara: Or perhaps you could get some new furniture. If you do, I'd suggest looking for things that don't need so much space. Some of those you have now, like that desk, are too big for the room, really.

Leon: (4) <u>No, I don't agree with you about that.</u> I need quite a big desk top for my computer and all the things that go with it, as well as something to write on. There's all that homework I have to do.

Zara: Yes, I suppose so. But there are other things you could do.

Leon: Such as?

Zara: Well, you get a lot of sunshine coming in through the window, so how about putting a big mirror on the wall opposite?

Leon: Hmm. You may be right. It would make the place a lot brighter, particularly in winter. (5) <u>Yes, I think I'll do that.</u> Let's go shopping on Saturday morning!

Writing Part 1

1 on **2** hardly **3** has/has got (consists of) **4** a little
5 at (during, over, on – US English)

Vocabulary

Across: **6** drawers **7** pillow **9** garage **11** balcony
12 cooker **13** bulb **14** blanket **16** mirror **17** sink

Down: **1** corridor **2** sofa **3** microwave **4** cushion
5 hall **8** washbasin **10** armchair **13** bell **15** tap

Vocabulary Extra
House and home

❶ a **1** wall **2** kitchen **3** dining room **4** hall
5 stairs **6** roof **7** ceiling **8** bedroom
9 living room **10** bathroom **11** lavatory
12 chimney

b (order of diagrams)
bedroom: alarm clock, duvet, sheets, hairdryer
bathroom: shower
kitchen: freezer, kettle, frying pan

c Suggested answers:
bedroom: bed, chest of drawers, blankets
bathroom: bath, toilet/WC/lavatory, wash basin
kitchen: fridge, washing machine, cooker

❷ a **Countable:** windmills, dishes, caves, flats, switches, bins, plugs, curtains, cottages, blinds, steps, shelves
Uncountable: heating, furniture, food, shampoo, make-up, sunshine, housework, money, cleaning, electricity, air-conditioning

b Suggested answers
   Countable: blankets, apartments, stairs
   Uncountable: snow, time, water

Unit 2

Listening Part 1

1 C **2** B **3** A **4** A **5** B

Recording script   CD1 Track 2

Announcer: Example. What did the boy use to wear to school?

Girl: Don't you have to wear a uniform to school, Adam?

Boy: Not any more. I'm so glad I don't have to wear a tie any more like I did in my old school. Now I can wear anything I like except we're not allowed to wear hats.

Girl: I think boys look much smarter in jackets and ties.

Announcer: One. What is included in the cost of the school theatre trip?

Boy: Are the tickets expensive for the theatre trip?

Girl: Well. They're 7.50 which isn't bad. But you'll need another £1.75 for the bus fare.

Boy: What about food?

Girl: We get a free ice cream in the interval but we'll be having lunch at school before we leave so you won't need any money for that.

Announcer: Two. What time will school finish today?

Teacher: OK, listen everyone. I've got an important announcement to make. Because of the bad weather school will finish half an hour earlier today. Afternoon lessons will begin at 2.15 instead of 2.30 and end at 3.30 instead of 4 o'clock. After-school activities at 4.30 have been cancelled. The school office has informed your parents about this. OK? Right …

Announcer: Three. What's the quickest way to get to the boy's school?

Boy: My mum sometimes gives me a lift to school but we often get held up in traffic and it can take up to 45 minutes to get there. So I actually prefer cycling because that only takes 20 minutes and I can spend longer having breakfast. The Underground would be quickest if I lived nearer the station. But it takes me at least 15 minutes to walk there.

Announcer: Four. What must the girl do at 1.30?

Girl: Listen, I'll meet you in the changing rooms at 1.45 for hockey practice because at half past one I've got to see Mrs Alan – she's lending me a book for my Geography course work. So it's twenty past one now so I've just got time to take my books back to the library. See you later.

Announcer: Five. When will the boy have a maths test?

Boy: So the maths test is on the 25th, isn't it?

Teacher: That's a Saturday, so it's the day before.

Boy: So Friday the 24th. That's only a week away.

Teacher: Don't worry. I've arranged a revision lesson for your class to do some extra test practice on the 23rd and you've got all weekend to study.

Reading Part 3

1 A **2** B **3** A **4** A **5** A **6** B

Vocabulary

1 failed; take   **2** study; make   **3** missed; spend
4 had; made   **5** study; lose   **6** learn; spend
7 spend; take   **8** miss; take   **9** lost   **10** made

Grammar

❶ 1 used to go   **2** wasn't; was doing   **3** phoned; was walking   **4** was studying; was crying   **5** met; was waiting   **6** didn't finish; wasn't listening   **7** didn't use to like   **8** were playing; fell over

❷ 1 What g   **2** Was c   **3** Did a   **4** Who b   **5** What f   **6** Did h   **7** How d   **8** When e

Writing Part 2

❷ a, d, e, g, h could be included in the email.

❸ All the main points are included. *I hope you will be able to play in the next match* is unnecessary information.

❹ The email is too long. The maximum number of words is 45.

With best wishes is too formal. You would use this to write to a teacher or another adult you don't know very well. He could use *See you soon*! or *Take care*.

❻ Possible **answer**:

Hi Anna

I'm sorry that I couldn't come shopping with you yesterday but I had too much French homework. Did you have a good shopping trip? Can I come to your house tomorrow to see what you bought?

Let me know.

Tina (42 words)

Vocabulary Extra

Daily life

❶ **1** ate **2** bought **3** drove **4** had **5** left **6** learnt
7 lost **8** rang **9** spent **10** took

❷

do	make	have	spend	earn
sport	breakfast	breakfast	money	money
a job	money	a break	time	a wage
homework	a suggestion	a job		
	friends	fun		
	a decision	money		
		time		
		friends		

❹ **1** B **2** C **3** D **4** A **5** C **6** D **7** B **8** C

Unit 3

Reading Part 4

1 A **2** B **3** D **4** B

Grammar

❶ **2** to lend → lending **3** play → to play **4** to spend
→ spending **5** buying → to buy **6** be → to be
7 to miss → missing **8** stay → staying **9** taking →
to take **10** doing → to do

❷ **1** a correct; b correct **2** a bringing → to bring; b
correct **3** a turning off → to turn off; b buying → to
buy **4** a correct; b correct **5** a to go → going; b to
watch → watching **6** a correct; b to see → seeing

Listening Part 2

1 A **2** C **3** A **4** B **5** C **6** A

Recording script CD1 Track 3

Interviewer: So tell me, Ben, what made you start collecting picture postcards?

Ben: As a boy I often saw postcards at the seaside and in tourist places, but I didn't find them interesting then. (1) <u>That suddenly changed a few years ago when I discovered hundreds of them</u> in the spare room. There were some beautiful ones there, carefully arranged in albums. So after that I started collecting cards whenever I went to other countries.

Interviewer: Whose collection was it?

Ben: Well, my grandfather, who was a sailor, used to send postcards home from wherever he was in the world. Anyway my mum and my uncle, who were both kids at the time, would always read them, and (2) <u>she decided to keep them all. So that's how the family collection began.</u>

Interviewer: Which kind of postcards do you like best these days?

Ben: Well, I still like the ones with pictures of famous harbours, like Sydney and New York. And I've also got some that have beautiful photos of cathedrals and mosques, but (3) <u>most of all I love the ones which show ships, trains and planes from early last century.</u>

Interviewer: What do you think of those old comic postcards?

Ben: They're fascinating. Some of the pictures were actually drawn by top-class comic artists, real professionals. And what makes me laugh is not the jokes themselves – they're really awful – but just (4) <u>how out-of-date they seem now. They tell us a lot about how differently people saw things in those days.</u>

Interviewer: Yes, they give us an idea of what society was like back then. Some of the very old ones must be quite valuable nowadays.

Ben: Yes, though perhaps surprisingly (5) <u>it's the subject of the picture that matters most,</u> not because it's from the end of the 19th century, or whether it's been posted or not. <u>The ones with the highest values are about past events,</u> like a famous wedding, or a football team winning the cup – that kind of thing.

Interviewer: So for a young person, say, who wants to take up collecting postcards, those aren't the best kind to get?

Ben: No, they'd cost far too much. The same is true for cards with pictures of the town where you grew up – everyone wants them, so the prices are high. It's much better to go to a shop or street market and (6) <u>buy a variety of postcards, maybe a whole box of them.</u> Those can be amazingly cheap, and you never know what you might find there.

Writing Part 1

1 breathing **2** forward to **3** going **4** afford to
5 prefer camping

Vocabulary

Across: **2** cyclist **4** helmet **6** fee **7** surf **10** book
11 cook **12** dive **13** healthy

Down: **1** value **2** chess **3** tent **5** afford **6** fancy
8 bike **9** camera **10** brush

Vocabulary Extra

Hobbies and free time

1 a A cycling   B surfing   C camping
D (playing) music

b 1 e   2 f   3 i   4 b   5 d   6 h   7 l   8 g   9 j
10 a   11 k   12 c

2 unfair, untrue, unfit, unlucky, unkind, unhealthy, unknown, untidy

incorrect, incomplete, independent, informal, indirect

impatient, impossible, impolite, imperfect, improbable

3 1 f   2 e   3 g   4 b   5 h   6 c   7 a   8 d

UNIT 4

Reading Part 3

1 A   2 B   3 B   4 A   5 A   6 B   7 B   8 B

Listening Part 3

1 9.30   2 jacket   3 shopping   4 painting   5 1894
6 houses

Recording script   CD1 Track 4

OK, so tomorrow we'll be doing a tour of the city to see some of the most important sights in San Francisco. Now, we need to be at the Ferry Building in time to catch the ferry at 10am. But I think we should aim to be there by 9.45. It's a fifteen-minute walk from the hotel, so we should set off from here (1) <u>at 9.30</u>. You won't need to bring any money for food because a packed lunch is provided. It should be sunny tomorrow but it can get windy on the ferry, so I'd advise you to take (2) <u>a jacket.</u>

The ferry crosses the bay to Sausalito, which takes about 25 minutes. We'll spend about an hour in Sausalito where we'll do some (3) <u>shopping.</u> That's one of Sausalito's main attractions.

From Sausalito we'll get a bus across the Golden Gate Bridge to the Golden Gate Park. Here you'll have a choice of activities. Firstly, the de Young Museum. The best thing here is the (4) <u>painting collection</u>. This has some of the greatest works from every period in American history. The de Young's also famous for its collections of modern sculpture and African art.

Or you can go to the Japanese Tea Garden. This is the oldest Japanese garden in the United States. It first opened in (5) <u>1894</u> as part of an international exhibition. Anyway, you'll have about an hour to explore either of these two places before we break for lunch.

Our first stop after lunch will be at Alamo Square. I'm sure this will seem familiar to many of you as the (6) <u>houses</u> have appeared in so many films and TV shows. We'll stop and take some photos here before moving on to Chinatown where we'll have a guided walking tour.

Grammar

1 1 different; Moscow is the biggest city in Europe.
2 same
3 different; There aren't many ports in the world that are as busy as Shanghai.
4 different; The Burj Dubai is much taller than the CN tower.
5 different; You need to pay more to live on Avenue Princess Grace than on Fifth Avenue.
6 same

2 1 safest   2 noisier   3 hilliest   4 best   5 heavier
6 big   7 better   8 further   9 wettest   10 dangerous

Vocabulary

1 1 terrible   2 fascinating   3 boring   4 cheap
5 expensive   6 warm   7 freezing   8 crowded
9 filthy   10 fantastic

2 **very**: boring, cheap, expensive, warm, crowded, noisy
really: all of them
absolutely/extremely: terrible, fascinating, freezing, filthy, fantastic

3 Students' own answers.

4 1 police station – e   2 youth club – d   3 stadium – c
4 factory – f   5 tourist office – a   6 art gallery – b

Writing Part 3

a Yes   **b** Yes   **c** No. All his sentences are short and simple.   **d** No. He uses one comparative and one superlative structure, which is good. But he only uses the present simple tense. **e** No. He only uses basic adjectives and he repeats 'I like' several times.

Vocabulary Extra

Describing places

1 1 souvenirs 2 snorkelling 3 snowboarding
4 trekking 5 photos 6 sightseeing

2 1 F 2 C 3 A 4 D 5 E 6 B

3 1 enormous 2 shallow 3 boiling 4 hilly 5 dull
6 dangerous

4 1 modern; crowded 2 expensive; big
3 fantastic; terrible 4 dirty; narrow
5 enormous; wonderful 6 interesting; cheap
7 noisy; dangerous 8 lively; nice

Unit 5

Reading Part 5

1 A 2 B 3 C 4 A 5 C 6 D 7 D 8 B 9 A 10 B

Vocabulary

1 2 bored 3 correct 4 correct 5 exciting 6 correct
7 relaxed 8 frightening 9 correct 10 annoyed

2 a

1	C	H	E	E	R	F	U	L	
2					N	E	R	V	O	U	S
3	D	E	P	R	E	S	S	E	D
4				R	E	L	A	X	E	D
5		P	O	S	I	T	I	V	E
6					N	E	G	A	T	I	V	E
7	D	E	L	I	G	H	T	E	D
8			D	I	S	A	P	P	O	I	N	T	E	D

2 b cheerful/depressed, nervous/relaxed, positive/
negative, delighted/disappointed

Listening Part 4

1 A 2 B 3 B 4 B 5 A 6 A

Grammar

1 1 we can't 2 we should 3 I mustn't/can't 4 we might not 5 I don't have to 6 we should 7 It might be 8 I/we/you don't have to 9 we shouldn't 10 I should

2 2 might 3 mustn't 4 can't 5 should 6 may 7 don't have to 8 must 9 Could 10 have to

3 1 correct 2 has to → could/may/might 3 might → must 4 correct 5 ought to → have to 6 don't have to → shouldn't 7 correct 8 might → must 9 mustn't → don't have to 10 can → may/might/could/must

Writing Part 3

1 Yes. Parts of it are too formal.

2 I have received → Thanks for; I apologise to you → Sorry; extremely enjoyable → great!; I have no further information to add at the present time → Well, that's all for now; I look forward to hearing from you → Please write soon; Yours sincerely → Best wishes

Vocabulary Extra

Feelings

1 a 1 jealous 2 upset 3 amused 4 impatient 5 lazy 6 curious 7 ashamed 8 confident 9 nervous 10 pleased

b **Suggested answers:** Positive – amused, confident, pleased.
Negative – jealous, upset, impatient, lazy, ashamed, nervous.
Neither positive nor negative – curious.

2 1 of 2 about 3 about 4 with 5 of 6 with 7 with 8 about 9 of 10 about

3 a 1 rude 2 intelligent 3 mean 4 kind 5 boring 6 cheerful

b 1 rude: negative, polite: positive 2 intelligent: positive, stupid: negative 3 mean: negative, generous: positive 4 kind: positive, cruel: negative 5 boring: negative, interesting: positive 6 cheerful: positive, miserable: negative

UNIT 6

Reading Part 2

1 A 2 C 3 E 4 G 5 F

Vocabulary

1 a quiz show b chat show c comedy series d cartoon e documentary f the news

2 1 review 2 subtitles 3 interval 4 performance 5 venue 6 live 7 admission 8 audience

Listening Part 1

1 B 2 C 3 A 4 C 5 B

Recording script CD1 Track 6

Announcer: Example. What did the boy use to wear to school?

Girl: Don't you have to wear a uniform to school, Adam?

Boy: Not any more. I'm so glad I don't have to wear <u>a tie any more like I did in my old school.</u> Now I can wear anything I like except we're not allowed to wear hats.

Girl: I think boys look much smarter in jackets and ties.

Announcer: One. What has the boy just bought?

Girl: Are you enjoying that <u>book</u>?

Boy: Yes. I think I like it better than the film – I saw it for the first time on DVD a few weeks ago and then yesterday I saw it on sale in the bookshop, so I decided to get it.

Girl: I really like the music. I'll make a copy of the CD if you like.

Boy: Yes. That'd be great. Thanks.

Announcer: Two. What does Rachel need to get for the party?

Anne: Have you decided what you're wearing to the party, Rachel?

Rachel: Well, I'm borrowing my sister's skirt but I haven't got <u>a top that matches. I think a sleeveless one</u> would look best.

Anne: We could go shopping tomorrow. I need to get some earrings and a bag.

Rachel: I'll lend you some earrings if you like. My silver ones would look nice with your dress.

Announcer: Three. What is Kerry wearing?

Kerry: Hi, Matt. Have you seen Kerry? She was here a minute ago.

Matt:	I don't think I know Kerry. What does she look like?
Kerry:	She's got blond hair and she's wearing a pink and red T-shirt.
Matt:	Is it striped?
Kerry:	It's got a pattern on it. It's short-sleeved with a v-neck.
Matt:	Sorry. I've only seen a blond girl with a long-sleeved T-shirt.
Announcer:	Four. What does the reviewer recommend on TV this evening?
Reviewer:	This evening, chat show host Martin Wheeler interviews Fay West. Martin fails to get answers to the important questions so if I were you I'd watch the documentary on Channel 3 instead. It's about the fashion industry in India – full of surprising information and very entertaining. The new series of the cartoon *Strawberry Jam* starts tonight – many fans will find this hugely disappointing after the success of the last series.
Announcer:	Five. What time does the film start?
Woman:	Shall we have a drink before the film starts?
Man:	Yes, the café in the cinema is quite nice. I'll meet you there at half past eight.
Woman:	That doesn't give us much time before the film. I don't want to miss the start.
Man:	Oh yes, it's at quarter to nine, isn't it? They usually start at 9. All right. I'll see you in the café at 8.15.

Grammar

❶ 1 for 2 already 3 just 4 since 5 yet 6 already 7 just 8 yet 9 for 10 since

❷ 1 stayed 2 hasn't decided 3 read 4 have visited 5 watched 6 have known 7 haven't worn 8 became

Writing Part 2

❶ grammatically incorrect: a, c, f
has a punctuation mistake: e – Let's see *Twilight*. (no question mark)
OK: b, d, g, h
Other phrases for making suggestions and offers:
We could go to see *Twilight*. How about going to see *Twilight*?
I'll book the tickets if you like.

❷ Suggested answer

Dear Isabel

We could go to see 'Twilight'. I've heard it's a very good film and I really like the main actor. If you like, I could book the tickets for us both.

I'll phone you when I've got more information.

Tania

Vocabulary Extra

TV and clothes

❶ 1 B 2 A 3 E 4 C 5 F 6 D

❷ 1 backpack 2 wallet 3 earring 4 button 5 sweater 6 pocket 7 handbag 8 purse

❸ 1 E 2 F 3 B 4 A 5 C 6 D

Unit 7

Reading Part 1

1 A 2 B 3 C 4 B 5 B

Grammar

❶ 1 correct 2 I go → I'm going to buy 3 I don't will be → I won't be 4 I'm going to do → am I going to do 5 correct 6 You didn't going to → you aren't going to 7 shall be better → will be better 8 correct 9 we'll meet → we're meeting 10 I'm going to buy → I'll buy

❷ 1 is going to reach 2 gets 3 're meeting 4 will 5 'll go 6 're having 7 'll have to 8 're going 9 leaves 10 'll have 11 'll post 12 reaches

Writing Part 1

1 minutes by / in the 2 out of 3 go on 4 usually warm enough 5 probably won't

Listening Part 2

Answers: 1 B 2 B 3 A 4 C 5 A 6 C

Recording script CD1 Track 7

Man:	How did you become a weather forecaster, Charlotte, and when did you start doing TV forecasts?
Woman:	Well, I studied physics for four years at university, then spent six months on a weather training course. I worked at the local weather centre for a while, until about five years ago I got a job with the BBC doing weather forecasts. (1) I actually started doing them on television three years ago, after two years giving radio forecasts. I really enjoy the work.

Man:	What do you like best about it?
Woman:	I feel (2) <u>I'm helping those who need to know what the weather's going to be like.</u> Sometimes we get letters from farmers, thanking us for what we're doing. And I know how important the forecast is to people going out in small boats, because my favourite hobby is sailing.
Man:	Does it make many people change their plans, or decide not to travel?
Woman:	Oh yes. Those flying small aeroplanes, for instance. They often choose their route according to the forecast. And people planning journeys by road want to know if there's going to be fog or heavy snow so they can set out earlier. (3) <u>Or not go at all,</u> if conditions are really bad. And the forecast can warn those taking the train to expect delays.
Man:	So with all those people depending on you, the forecast has to be right, doesn't it?
Woman:	Yes, and these days we normally get it right for the following day around 85% of the time. And (4) <u>most of the time we can say what it's going to be like three days into the future,</u> too. 30 years ago we could only say what the weather would be like one day ahead, but now we sometimes get it right for the whole week. We have weather balloons and photos taken from space, and of course computers.
Man:	All that must make your job a lot easier.
Woman:	Well, (5) <u>yes and no. Certainly it helps you produce more accurate forecasts, but it also creates a huge amount of extra work for us.</u> You only appear on TV for a few minutes every day, but you spend hours studying all this information and preparing the forecasts.
Man:	And what do people say when they recognise you? In the street, say.
Woman:	Well, nearly everyone is really friendly. I think (6) <u>they realise that with weather like ours it's quite hard to be right all the time.</u> I mean, it can be sunny at one end of the street and raining heavily at the other end. But occasionally you meet someone who says, 'You were wrong again', even if you weren't, and that can be fairly annoying. And just the other week a man in a shop said to me, 'I never watch the weather forecast because you're always wrong'. So I replied, 'If you never watch it, how do you know?' He couldn't answer that!

Vocabulary

❶ 40+: very (hot), extremely (hot), 30–40: fairly (hot), rather (hot), quite (hot)

❷ 2 on/onto, off, by, train   3 on/onto, off, by, plane
4 in/into, out of, by, car   5 on/onto, off, by, bike
6 on, foot

❸ **Across:** 3 seasons   4 sunny   5 umbrella   7 traffic
10 signpost   11 extremely

Down: 1 showers   2 stormy   4 scooter   6 rails
8 rather   9 foggy

Vocabulary Extra

Weather and transport

❶ 1 suitcase F   2 motorbike J   3 signpost B
4 underground D   5 guidebook A   6 crossroads E
7 hitchhiker I   8 backpack C   9 roundabout G
10 railway H

❷ 1 railway   2 guidebook   3 backpack   4 crossroads
5 hitchhike   6 signpost

Suggested answers: Before the journey, I put my clothes tidily in my *suitcase*.
My brother has always wanted a *motorbike* but my parents won't let him have one.
The trains on the *underground* run through tunnels below the city.
We went around the *roundabout* and took the third road on the right.

❸ 1 temperature, degrees   2 clouds, cloudy   3 sun, sunny   4 wind, windy   5 rain, raining   6 snow, snowing   7 lightning, thunder   8 frost, icy

Unit 8

Vocabulary

❶ 1 granddaughter   2 brother-in-law   3 twins   4 sister
5 aunt   6 father-in-law   7 uncle   8 sons
9 grandchildren   10 nephews

❷ 1 get on with   2 taken up   3 set up   4 look after
5 find out   6 made up   7 grow up   8 brought up

Reading Part 3

1 B   2 A   3 A   4 B   5 B   6 A   7 B   8 B   9 A   10 A

Grammar

❶ 1 c   2 f   3 d   4 a   5 b   6 h   7 e   8 g

❷ 1 feel; won't   2 were; would enjoy   3 grows; he'll
4 get; I'll   5 lived; I'd   6 stops; we'll   7 had; I'd
8 have; helps

❸ Possible answers:

1 If I lived in the country, I would grow all my own vegetables. If I lived in the city, I would sell my car.
2 If I had more time, I would play tennis every day.
3 If I have a problem, I usually speak to my best friend.
4 When I'm older, I will open a chocolate shop.
5 If it rains this weekend, I will go to the cinema.
6 Unless I work hard, I won't get to university.

Listening Part 3

1 17th July   **2** 16   **3** hard-working   **4** confident
5 travel expenses   **6** Willoughby

Recording script CD1 Track 8

Now I've got some information about an exciting opportunity that I'm sure some of you will be interested in. The Association of Firefighters is organising a special programme this summer to teach girls how to become firefighters. It's being run at the Tacoma Firefighting Center for one week, from (1) July 17th to July 22nd.

There's only room for 24 students and it's expected there will be strong competition for places. Last year they received over 100 applications. This course is only open to students who are aged between (2) 16 and 18 and you'll have the chance to train alongside professional female firefighters. Although there've been female firefighters since 1973, only 2% of the 300,000 firefighters in the US and Canada are women. The organisers are looking for students who are both (3) hard-working and in good physical shape, although there aren't any height requirements.

Now you don't have to necessarily be thinking about joining the fire service when you leave school in order to do the course. Everyone benefits because the skills you learn will make you more (4) confident.

You don't have to pay for the cost of the course but you will have to cover the cost of your (5) travel expenses. I hope some of you will consider applying. If you are interested you need to contact Elaine (6) Willoughby, that's W I DOUBLE L O U G H B Y at Central Fire Station. You should contact her before Wednesday next week on 099898765.

Right. That's all I've got to say ...

Writing Part 2

❶ Spelling mistakes in italics and underlined; punctuation mistakes underlined.

Dear Fred

The wedding was good _because_ it was in a _beautiful_ hotel near the beach. The food was _excellent_. Aunt Emilia's husband is _quite_ handsome but a little bit bald! What do you think of these photos? I look the best, don't I?!

Take care,

Ricardo

Vocabulary Extra
Describing people

❶ **1** thin   **2** bald   **3** moustache   **4** scar
5 straight   **6** dark   **7** looks   **8** smart   **9** medium
10 broad   **11** curly   **12** fair / blonde   **13** blonde / fair   **14** wavy

❷ **1** hard-working   **2** smart   **3** noisy   **4** mean   **5** rude
6 calm   **7** confident   **8** warm

❸ **1** friendly   **2** cheerful   **3** unreliable   **4** selfish
5 dishonest   **6** reliable   **7** impatient   **8** childish

Unit 9
Listening Part 4

1 A   **2** A   **3** B   **4** B   **5** A   **6** B

Recording script CD1 Track 9

Abbie:	I love tennis, but there's so much to learn, isn't there, Mike?
Mike:	Yes, Abbie, but you already know a lot of the basic things.
Abbie:	Such as?
Mike:	Well, like standing in the right place in the court. And (1) where the racket is in your hand. That's fine.
Abbie:	But there's so much more to it than that, isn't there? I mean, all the different ways of hitting the ball, being in exactly the right place at the right time. On TV you can see the big tennis stars doing the most amazing things...
Mike:	Actually, (2) it's quite a good idea to do that. You can learn a lot from the way they play.
Abbie:	But the top players move around the court so fast, don't they? (3) I'll never be able to do that.
Mike:	I can't see why not, with the right training.
Abbie:	Well, for one thing I couldn't run around for hours the way they do. At that speed, I'd be too tired to move after about 20 minutes!

Mike:	At the moment, that's probably true. But let's see in a couple of years.
Abbie:	So what should I do next? Put my name down for competitions?
Mike:	Well, I think (4) <u>for now it'd be better just to keep playing at school and with friends.</u> And I can start giving you lessons from next week, if you like. Let's see how you get on for a while and then maybe we'll think about matches.
Abbie:	Sounds great.
Mike:	I'll give you a book to read about tennis. It's got lots of useful advice in it, and the rules of the sport. (5) <u>You should make sure you know all those.</u>
Abbie:	<u>Right. I'll look at them carefully.</u> I didn't actually know until you told me that players aren't allowed to touch the net!
Mike:	And I suggest you work on your general fitness, too.
Abbie:	OK, (6) <u>I'll definitely run or train down at the gym each evening, except Sundays.</u> I think you need a break sometime, don't you?
Mike:	Yes, you do. That's very important.

Grammar

1 1 d 2 g 3 f 4 h 5 a 6 e 7 b 8 c

2 a 1 who 2 that 3 who 4 which 5 where
6 whose 7 when 8 which 9 when 10 whose
11 where 12 that

b 4, 9

Reading Part 5

1 C 2 A 3 D 4 B 5 A 6 B 7 C 8 C 9 A 10 C

Vocabulary

1 1 competition 2 court 3 bat 4 net 5 breath
6 energy 7 injury 8 treatment

2 Across: 1 symptom 2 fit 5 cough 7 cold 8 bruise
12 patient 14 tablet 15 disease

Down: 1 sick 3 ill 4 ache 6 hurt 9 sore
10 healthy 11 injure 12 pill 13 nurse

Writing Part 3

1 1 teacher, story 2 your English teacher 3 *The missing case,* at the top (the title) 4 you can choose

2 1 had been containing → contained 2 that made me → which made me 3 at its place → in its place

3 1 A little long, but that's better than too short!
2 yes 3 yes 4 *but, so, if, after, yet, when* 5 yes
6 quite good 7 a mystery: we don't know what was in the bag, what happened to it, or what the boss said or did.

Vocabulary Extra

Sports and health

1 a 1 b 2 a 3 f 4 d 5 c 6 e

b go swimming; do gymnastics, boxing, athletics; play basketball, football

Suggested answers:

go cycling/running/jogging/surfing/skiing/windsurfing/climbing/riding

do the long jump/the high jump/fitness training/shooting/water sports

play golf/tennis/volleyball/squash/hockey/baseball/rugby/table tennis

2 1 shorts 2 boots 3 trainers 4 helmet 5 racket
6 gloves

Suggested answers:

1 shorts: football, athletics, volleyball **2** boots: climbing, rugby, hockey **3** trainers: basketball, jogging, fitness training **4** helmet: cycling, motor-cycling, motor-racing **5** racket: tennis, squash, badminton **6** gloves: skiing, ice hockey, boxing

3 a win/won/won; lose/lost/lost; draw/drew/drawn; beat/beat/beaten, score/scored/scored; hit/hit/hit; kick/kicked/kicked

b 2 hit 3 win 4 kick 5 beat 6 lose 7 throw
8 draw

4 2 d 3 g 4 f 5 h 6 a 7 b 8 e

Unit 10

Reading Part 2

1 D 2 E 3 A 4 C 5 G

Grammar

1 1 How often do you have your hair cut?
2 When did you last have your teeth checked?
3 How often do you have your photo taken?
4 When did you last have your eyes tested?
5 How often do you get your mobile phone replaced?
6 When did you last have your bedroom painted?
7 When did you last get your computer fixed?
8 How often do you get your passport changed?

2 1 gets 2 is having 3 had 4 gets 5 had
6 is having 7 are getting 8 had

Vocabulary

1 C 2 H 3 A 4 F 5 G 6 B 7 E 8 D

Listening Part 1

1 B 2 B 3 C 4 A 5 C 6 A 7 B

Recording script CD1 Track 10

Announcer: Example. What did the boy use to wear to school?

Girl: Don't you have to wear a uniform to school, Adam?

Boy: Not any more. I'm so glad I don't have to wear a tie any more like I did in my old school. Now I can wear anything I like except we're not allowed to wear hats.

Girl: I think boys look much smarter in jackets and ties.

Announcer: One. What does the woman need?

Man: Shall I get a loaf of bread while I'm out?

Woman: It's OK, I got one this morning. But I did forget to get toothpaste.

Man: Fine. What about a tin of tomatoes? We've run out of those as well.

Woman: There's some in the basement, so don't worry.

Announcer: Two. What time is the girl's appointment?

Father: Your dentist's appointment's at half past ten, isn't it, Jo?

Jo: I thought it was at eleven. Let me check. No. You're right. It was at half past ten and then they changed it to quarter to eleven.

Father: OK. I'll pick you up from school after the break.

Announcer: Three. What did the man have to eat in the restaurant?

Helen: What did you have to eat in the restaurant, David?

David: Well, I couldn't decide between the steak and the fish.

Helen: That restaurant is well known for its barbecues.

David: Yes, but I went for the cod in the end. It was really good. The others had ham and that was good too.

Announcer: Four. What kind of fruit does the girl decide to buy?

Seller: What can I get you? These strawberries are lovely. Try one.

Customer: Mmm. They are nice but a bit expensive.

Seller: Right. Well, there's pineapple. These ones are very juicy.

Customer: I'm not very keen on pineapple. What about melon?

Seller: I'd take the strawberries. The melons aren't ripe enough yet.

Customer: OK.

Announcer: Five. What has the man had done?

Woman: So how's the house coming along?

Man: Well, I've had all the old windows replaced.

Woman: Why? They weren't broken, were they?

Man: Some of them were and they were so dirty.

Woman: You'll need to get them painted before the winter.

Man: I'll do that myself.

Announcer: Six. What is the woman complaining about?

Woman: I'm just ringing to let you know how disappointed I was with the standards in the hotel. Our bathroom didn't look like it'd been cleaned when we arrived and our bed was never made until the afternoon. I've got no complaints about the food or the facilities. The pool, for example, was better than I expected.

Announcer: Seven. What does the boy want to borrow?

Chris: Hello, Mrs Lane. Sorry to disturb you. I'm cooking a special dinner for my parents tonight and I need another frying pan. I'm cooking lots of fish.

Mrs Lane: Oh, that's no problem, Chris. Have you got a big serving dish to put it on?

Chris: Yes. I think so.

Mrs Lane: OK. Be very careful with the knife when you're cutting the fish, won't you?

Writing Part 2

❶ Correct sentences = c, d, e, g, h, k

❷ Possible answer:

Dear Tom

I'm sorry I recommended Barney's. Last time it was very good but perhaps the chef has left. I will take you to a better pizza restaurant next time I see you. When would you like to go?

See you soon,

Maria

4 1 neither Martha nor Stefano say WHEN they suggest going to the restaurant.

2 Both are about 45 words long.

3 Stefano writes 'See you soon'.

4 Martha: favourite, excellent, spaghetti

5 Martha: missing capital letter: *The food...* and *They are great.*
Stefano: Missing capital letter and comma: *...Also, it has* .

6 Martha: wrong verb pattern: *I hope you will answer me* (although it would be more natural to say *I hope you'll let me know soon*); *spaghetti* is uncountable.
Stefano: wrong pronoun: *their desserts* and *their ice cream.*

7 Martha: pizza, pasta, spaghetti, sandwiches.

Vocabulary Extra

Food, house and home

S	F	R	Y	I	N	G	P	A	N
H	O	H	A	M	I	R	L	A	G
A	K	E	T	T	L	E	S	K	U
M	N	G	F	O	R	K	L	N	L
M	I	R	N	U	A	N	P	I	P
E	V	I	N	D	R	I	E	F	I
R	H	A	I	R	D	R	Y	E	R
O	J	U	N	K	E	T	E	L	O
F	R	Y	P	O	T	Y	E	C	N

2 1 F   2 A   3 B   4 E   5 D   6 G   7 H   8 C

3 2 bars of soap
a bar of chocolate
some slices of cheese
a jar of honey
a tube of toothpaste
a loaf of bread
a carton/bottle of milk
4 bottles of water
a tin/can of tomatoes

4 1 food   2 meal   3 desserts   4 starter   5 dish
6 vegetarian

Unit 11

Reading Part 4

1 C   2 D   3 A   4 A   5 B

Grammar

1 2 was thrown out   3 was recycled   4 were left
5 were mixed   6 were shocked   7 was arranged
8 were made   9 are asked   10 is collected   11 are
separated   12 is used

2 1 were taken   2 were told   3 not allowed
4 were shown   5 are (usually) fed   6 was made
7 was (suddenly) approached   8 were seen
9 were (quickly) given   10 is ever attacked

Listening Part 2

1 C   2 C   3 A   4 B   5 A   6 B

> **Recording script**   CD1 Track 11
>
> It's amazing just how many nature programmes there are on TV. There are five good ones on in the next few days, starting with *Wildlife on Three* this evening. (1) This is actually on at half past seven, moved from its usual time of 6.45 because of the special news programme at six o'clock.
>
> Then, tomorrow afternoon, there's a new series starting: *India Live.* Over the coming weeks this will look at a whole range of wildlife, from the amazing creatures in India's many lakes and rivers to those up in the sky. (2) The first programme will concentrate on those old favourites, tigers, with some surprising film showing what good swimmers they are.
>
> That's at four thirty, followed later by *Desert Watch*, which this week tells us about plants that live in Chile's Atacama Desert despite the fact it hardly ever rains there. Scientists have discovered that even those far from the nearest river survive because of the fog that comes in from the cold Pacific Ocean. (3) The tiny drops of water in the damp, foggy atmosphere are just enough to keep them alive.
>
> On Wednesday there's a documentary about the failure of an environmental project on Macquarie Island, which lies halfway between Australia and Antarctica. Some years ago, they were worried that cats were a danger to its important bird population, so they removed all the cats. This increased the number of rabbits, which then (4) ate nearly all the plants on the island. Unfortunately, the birds need these to live, so now they'll have to do something about the rabbits.

There's another programme about man's effect on the environment on Friday, when Holly McShane finds out what's been happening down at the coast here. It seems that after centuries of trying to hold back the water by building higher and higher defences, they've now given up and (5) decided to allow the sea to flood in. The idea is to create an area of wetland for the local wildlife, and hope it will also attract birds from all over the world.

So why are there so many of these programmes on TV? The answer is that people like them. (6) It doesn't matter how old or how young they are, or when the programme is shown. It may be on early evening or later at night, and it could be about many different kinds of animals or just one. It makes little difference: lots of people will still want to watch it.

Writing Part 3

❶ 1 letter, penfriend   2 an English penfriend
3 that they've recently had a good holiday away from the city   4 where you like to go in your free time; whether your penfriend would like it there

❷ 1 ~~in~~ this year: preposition   2 prefer TO spend: verb form   3 usually choose: word order   4 next to A/ THE lake: article   5 beautiful: spelling   6 like TO swim: verb form   7 ON my holidays: preposition   8 different subjects: singular/plural   9 make trips → go on trips: vocabulary   10 National: spelling   11 You'll fall: verb form   12 looking forward to: word order.

❸ 1 Yes   2 Yes   3 The writer is happy that Liz enjoyed her holidays.   4 Yes. The first question is answered in paragraphs 2 and 3; the second in the last paragraph.   5 The writer tends to use only the simple present. The vocabulary used is adequate but not wide in range.   6 Hi ..., Thanks very much for..., I'm really pleased that...; I'm looking forward to hearing from you, Love.

Vocabulary

Across: 3 monkey   **7** fuel   **8** deer   **9** crocodile   **10** feed
12 pet   **17** elephant   **18** shark   **19** nature   **20** zebra

Down: 1 sun   **2** ice   **4** kangaroo   **5** wildlife   **6** bear
9 cage   **11** dolphin   **12** power   **13** tree   **14** forest
15 lion   **16** creature

Vocabulary Extra

Environment and the natural world

❶ 1 the Sun   2 the Earth   3 the moon   4 a planet
5 a star

❷ 1 forest   2 waterfall   3 lake   4 rock   5 mountain range   6 sand   7 river   8 hill   9 field   10 wave

❸ 1 wild   2 public   3 climate   4 solar   5 tropical
6 bottle   7 light   8 rubbish

❹ ⓐ –ion   2 –ment   3 -ation

ⓑ admiration, argument, celebration, communication, completion, conservation, creation, description, education, examination, explanation, invitation, pollution, preparation, pronunciation, registration, reservation, translation

UNIT 12

Reading Part 4

1 B   2 C   3 A   4 B   5 C

Grammar

❶ 1 he didn't/did not know

2 was going to take me/us to

3 they had/they'd never been

4 was sorry she hadn't/had not done her

5 Tom would phone me

6 they had/they'd finished university

7 he couldn't/could not remember where he'd/he had bought his

8 her laptop was broken, so she couldn't/could not send

❷ 1 'Go to bed!'

2 'Phone me as soon as you arrive.'

3 'Don't use my iPod, (Ellie)!'

4 'Don't worry about the exam!'

5 'Don't eat all the chocolate!'

❸ 1 often I listened

2 if/whether I preferred listening to the radio or to music on my iPod.

3 where and when I listened to the radio.

4 what the most popular radio station was in my town.

Listening Part 3

1 1964   **2** letters   **3** (some of the) DJs / deejays / disc jockeys   **4** 10 am–6 pm / from 10 am to 6 pm
5 June   **6** free

Recording script   CD1 Track 12

Now here's something for all you music lovers: a new exhibition to celebrate the pirate radio station Radio Caroline. For those of you too young to remember, it was called a pirate station because it was against the law and because it was based on a ship out at sea. Radio Caroline opened in (1) <u>1964</u> and was closed down four years later. At this time there were no other radio stations playing pop music for young people and it quickly became really popular.

The exhibition, as you would expect, includes the best-loved music from that time. There are original records by groups such as *The Beatles*, who actually visited Radio Caroline. You can also see some of the (2) <u>letters</u> sent by Radio Caroline's thousands of fans. It's also interesting to listen to the interviews with some of the (3) <u>DJs</u> who worked at Radio Caroline. They were very famous back then.

The exhibition is unusual because it's being held on the radio ship itself. It's open seven days a week from (4) <u>10 am to 6 pm.</u> You need to get there soon, though, because it only runs for eight weeks and will finish in (5) <u>June.</u> But there will be other events to celebrate Radio Caroline coming up soon. You won't need to buy a ticket because entry to the exhibition is (6) <u>free.</u> You can get more details from the website; www. …

Vocabulary

1 in front of   **2** behind   **3** over/across   **4** Opposite
5 on the right   **6** on the left   **7** inside/in   **8** between

Writing Part 3

❶ **1** Both stories have a clear ending, although story A is more successful at this.

2 Story B. Because of frequent punctuation and grammar errors, the reader has to make more effort to understand story A.

3 Story A: *they tell me it is my decicion, he said I can take the exam next week*
Story B: *I said my mother, she said hers*

4 Story A contains four punctuation mistakes.

5 Story A contains one spelling error.

6 Story A repeats *but* three times.
Story B repeats *so* and *but* several times.

7 Story B is too long (136 words).

---

❷ **Story A**
Spelling mistake: decicion → decision

Punctuation mistakes are <u>underlined</u>; grammar mistakes in **bold**:

In the first line I couldn't believe that it was the truth, but it <u>was!</u> **I had** won a prize of about ten thousand <u>American dollars.</u> <u>But</u> *(could replace with 'However,')* there was a <u>problem</u>. I needed to go personally to get the <u>prize</u>. <u>But</u> *(could replace with 'Unfortunately,')* it was the same date **as** my final **physics** exam! I didn't know what **I could do/to do**. I spoke with my parents and they **told** me that it **was** my decision. I spoke with my teacher and he said I **could** take the exam **the week after**.

Story B
I **said to / told** my mother I was sleeping at Ana's house and she **said to / told** hers she was sleeping at my house.

Vocabulary Extra

Social interaction and directions

❶ **1** tell   **2** communicate   **3** slang   **4** chat   **5** say   **6** texts
7 ask   **8** speak

❷

say:	hello, goodbye
tell:	lies, a joke, the truth, a story
speak:	the truth, a language, to friends
talk about:	plans, the answers, dreams, a story
ask for:	help, information, the truth, the answers

❸ **1** F   **2** T   **3** F   **4** F   **5** F   **6** F   **7** T   **8** T

Acknowledgements

The authors would like to thank Annabel Marriott, Judith Greet and Ann-Marie Murphy personally for all their hard work. Many thanks also to Chris Williams (Senior Production Controller), Michelle Simpson (Permissions Controller), Hilary Fletcher (Picture Researcher), John Green (Audio Producer), Tim Woolf (Audio Editor) and Kevin Doherty (Proof-reader).

Development of this publication has made use of the Cambridge International Corpus (CIC). The CIC is a computerised database of contemporary spoken and written English which currently stands at over one billion words. It includes British English, American English and other varieties of English. It also includes the Cambridge Learner Corpus, developed in collaboration with the University of Cambridge ESOL Examinations. Cambridge University Press has built up the CIC to provide evidence about language use that helps to produce better language teaching materials.

The authors and publishers acknowledge the following sources of copyright material and are grateful for the permissions granted. While every effort has been made, it has not always been possible to identify the sources of all the material used, or to trace all copyright holders. If any omissions are brought to our notice, we will be happy to include the appropriate acknowledgements on reprinting.

Channel Four Television Corporation for the text on p. 33 'Brat Camp' taken from the Channel 4 website; The text on p. 33 'The World's Strictest Parents is from the BBC.co.uk website; Manchester Evening News for the adapted article on p. 44 'My stay in the rainforest' from 'My Jungle Adventure' by Carmel Thompson, Manchester Evening News 17 July 2006.

For permission to reproduce photographs:

Key: l = left, c = centre, r = right, t = top, b = bottom, u = upper, lo = lower, f = far.

Action Plus/Steve Bardens p 38; Alamy/©Antiques & Collectables p 14 (l), /©Mary Evans Picture Library p 14 (tr), /©Amoret Tanner p 14 (bc), /©Photopat vintage p 14 (br), /©PCL p 17, /©Alvey & Towers Picture Library p 31 (bus, car), /©Elmtree Images p 31 (train), /©Michael Dwyer p 31 (plane), /©Kumar Sriskandan p 55 (tl), /©PhotoStock-Israel p 55 (bl); Corbis/©Adam Woolfitt p 16, /©Johannes Kroemer p 19, /©C. Devan p 22, /©Tracy Kahn p 32 (br), /©Robert Manella/Comstock p 40 (4), /©Jeffrey L. Rotman p 55 (tr), /©Ted Levin p 55 (cr); Getty Images/altrendo images p 32 (cfl), /Blend Images/Stewart Cohen p 23 (b), /DK Stock/Eric Glenn p 40 (3), /Iconica/Kevin Arnold p 31 (bike), /Iconica/Jose Luis Pelaez p 24 (2), /The Image Bank/Dreamlight p 31 (walk), /The Image Bank/Allison Michael Orenstein p 32 (cl), /Riser/Steve Baccon p 24 (3), /Riser/Don Klumpp p 32 (bc), /Riser/Bernhard Lang p 40 (2), /Photographer's Choice/Chemistry p 32 (cr), /Photographer's Choice/Sean Locke p 40 (1), /Stone/Steve Craft p 32 (cfr), /Stone/Peter Mason p 24 (1), /Stone/joSon p 24 (4), /Taxi/Lisa Peardon p 23 (t), /Workbook Stock/Jessica Miller p 32 (bl), /Workbook Stock/Michael Schmitt p 55 (cl), /Workbook Stock/Stephen Simpson p 11; Masterfile/Kevin Dodge p 40 (5); Photolibrary.com/Comstock/Creatas p 5, /Imagestate RM/Peter Thompson p 55 (br); Shutterstock Images/AVAVA p 24 (5), /Tommaso Lizzul p 48, /Monkey Business Images p 35, /Lisa F.Young p 32 (t).

Recordings produced by John Green, TEFL Tapes, edited by Tim Woolf, recorded at ID Audio, London.

Illustrations:

Carl Pearce pp. 8, 58 (tl), 61 (tl), 63
Aleksander Sotirovski pp. 8 (clocks), 26, 42, 57 (br), 61 (bl)
David Whamond pp. 4, 37, 45, 56
Andrew Painter pp. 6, 9, 50, 54
John Burns pp. 12, 59, 62 (tl)
Jake Lawrence pp. 20, 39, 57 (bl & tr), 60, 62 (bl)
Rob McClurkan pp. 52
Tracey Cox pp. 58 (br)

Cover design by Wild Apple Design Ltd

Designed and typeset by Wild Apple Design Ltd